The Common Core State Standards

in English Language Arts

for English Language Learners

Grades K–5

Pamela Spycher, Editor

The Common Core State Standards Series
Luciana C. de Oliveira, Series Editor

Typeset in Berkeley and News Gothic
by Capitol Communications. LLC, Crofton, Maryland USA
and printed by Gasch Printing, LLC, Odenton, Maryland USA

TESOL International Association
1925 Ballenger Avenue
Alexandria, Virginia 22314 USA
Tel 703-836-0774 • Fax 703-836-7864

Publishing Manager: Carol Edwards
Cover Design: Tomiko Breland
Project reviewer: Lynn Zimmerman

TESOL Book Publications Committee
               John I. Liontas, Chair
Robyn L. Brinks Lockwood, Co-chair   Guofang Li
Jennifer Lebedev   Deoksoon Kim
Gail Schafers   Gilda Martinez-Alba
Lynn Zimmerman   Adrian J. Wurr

ISBN 9781931185257
Library of Congress Control Number 2014930047

Contents

Introduction

Pamela Spycher, WestEd

This is an exciting time to be a teacher. The Common Core State Standards for English Language Arts and Literacy in History/Social Studies, Science, and Technical Subjects (CCSS for ELA/Literacy; National Governors Association Center for Best Practices & Council of Chief State School Officers, 2010) have invigorated the teaching profession and ushered in a new era of creativity, innovation, critical thinking, and collaboration, not only for students, but also for educators. While teachers across the nation are embracing this opportunity, they also recognize the challenges the CCSS for ELA/Literacy may present for educating children who are learning English as an additional language. Championing the idea of supporting English Learners' (ELs') simultaneous development of rich content knowledge and English makes intuitive sense. Creating powerful lessons and units of study that achieve this purpose is a bit more complicated. And yet, we expect nothing less of teachers.

All children have the right to a world-class education. This includes school experiences that are interactive and engaging, meaningful and relevant, and intellectually rich and challenging with intentional scaffolding that moves learners toward independence. A world-class education values students' primary languages and cultures as assets—valuable in their own right and resources to build upon for further learning. A world-class education supports students to develop deep content knowledge in science, history/social studies, English language arts, mathematics, the arts, and other content areas, as well as the advanced levels of language needed to interact meaningfully with others and with texts across the disciplines. This meaningful interaction could be via collaborative conversations where students share knowledge, ask for clarification or elaboration, and build on one another's ideas—all of which support deeper learning. It could be through analyzing and interpreting complex texts: digging deeper into the meanings of the texts and learning about how writers select and shape language purposefully to convey their ideas. Meaningful interactions can also be in the form of writing to represent one's understandings of the world, to entertain one's peers through a well-crafted story, or to persuade others to think a certain way or even to do something.

Whether or not ELs receive a world-class education depends in large part on their teachers' knowledge of pedagogy, content, and language, as well as their ability to reflect on and adapt their instructional practice to address the learning needs of their students. This volume was designed to deepen teachers' knowledge and provide practical instructional approaches for supporting kindergarten through fifth-grade ELs to meet the ambitious expectations set forth in the CCSS for ELA/Literacy. The chapters in this volume provide concrete ideas for engaging ELs in a range of intellectually rich tasks using a variety of text types to develop content knowledge and academic English simultaneously.

The second chapter, by Lems and Abousalem, focuses on the importance of immersing young ELs in the rich language and ideas of storybooks. In the primary grades, teacher storybook read-alouds are an ideal way to help ELs build oral language, vocabulary, and understandings about how literary texts work. The authors describe how Abousalem, a classroom teacher, provides many opportunities for her kindergarten and first-grade students to discuss a literary text and learn about the language in the text. In the third chapter, Merino, Fortes, Dubcovsky, and Galli-Banducci illustrate how a second/third-grade teacher, Rosa, enacted different types of scaffolding for her ELs through an inquiry-based science unit on snails. Merino et al. illustrate how Rosa facilitated students' understandings of descriptive language, beginning with a highly scaffolded stage and then moving through a "fading" stage and finally to a "transfer of responsibility" stage, where students were more independently able to observe and describe snails. Another layer in this chapter is that Rosa was conducting the science inquiry unit as her teacher research project in a teacher preparation course.

In Chapter 4, Capitelli, Alvarez, and Valdes provide a framework for understanding language demands and opportunities for embedding language development in instruction in an "Integrated Perspective on the Dimensions of School Communication." They demonstrate this perspective in action by describing lessons from a second-grade earth science unit and a fifth-grade U.S. history unit. They show how second-grade ELs develop vocabulary and use it meaningfully to orally describe the properties of rocks and compare and contrast different kinds of rocks, all the while deepening their understandings of the science concepts and preparing for writing. In the fifth-grade example, Capitelli et al. show how ELs worked collaboratively, first, to read a section of history text carefully using a focus question and, then, to determine which pieces of information were most pertinent to answering the focus question (*Who benefitted from the conflicts between Europeans and Native Americans?*). Through lively discussion and debate, the students prepared to write individual responses.

In the fifth chapter, Spycher and Linn-Nieves share approaches for supporting third–fifth graders to write various text types in integrated ELA and science. In this chapter, an organizing framework for planning units of study—the "teaching and learning cycle"—is explained. Spycher and Linn-Nieves demonstrate how ELs engage in a "text reconstruction" task in which they listen actively to a short informational text about bats, take notes on important words and phrases, discuss their notes with peers, and then collaboratively reconstruct the text. All the while, the students apply their understandings of how English works to make meaning and deepen their understandings of the topic. In Chapter 6, Garegnani shares how she raises her fourth- and fifth-grade ELs' language awareness through dialogue about the language features of different science text types. Through "scaffolded language analysis," Garegnani shows how, in the planning process, she analyzes the texts her students encounter for their language features and then discusses these features with her students in meaningful and highly interactive ways. It is through these interactive discussions about how the language of complex texts work that her ELs begin to gain confidence in understanding the language when they read and in producing similar language patterns themselves.

In Chapter 7, Levine discusses how ELs in third–fifth grade can be supported to read two different text types—an informational text about the circulatory system and a biography about a scientist—through three stages of a learning cycle: exploration, concept development, and application. Through these stages, Levine illustrates how multiple instructional approaches and strategies (e.g., questioning, sentence frames) can be used to support ELs to understand the texts and to begin using the language of the text types. August and Haynes present an approach for supporting ELs to read literary texts—Augmented Curriculum for ELLs, or ACE—in Chapter 8. In this chapter, fourth graders develop text-level, sentence-level, and word-level understandings through analysis of the texts they are reading in mainstream and supplemental lessons. These lessons address close-reading techniques, text-based evidence, writing from sources, and academic vocabulary. August and Haynes stress that supplemental mini-lessons should also address the particular learning needs of ELs, including attention to building background knowledge, vocabulary (e.g., cognate knowledge, morphology), and syntax, particularly where it concerns understanding the components of complex sentences.

In the ninth chapter, Mercuri and Yarussi share how they integrated language learning into an inquiry-based science unit on weather and weather changes in the fifth grade. In the 6-week-long unit, students engaged with the content knowledge in interactive ways (e.g., through several lab experiments) while they also learned about the characteristics of the text types used. Mercuri and Yarussi discuss how Yarussi, the classroom teacher, used multiple approaches to support her students' understandings of the science concepts and development of scientific literacy, including guiding her students to record their science experiment observations in lab reports and providing them with paragraph frames to discuss and write their findings. In Chapter 10, O'Loughlin provides a fresh take on the use of picture books to promote language and literacy development in integrated ELA and history/social science in fifth grade. O'Loughlin illustrates how using picture books for the study of historical topics helps the content "come alive" for ELs. Importantly, using picture books promotes language and literacy development and visual literacy, as the strategic use of visuals in picture books provides an opportunity for ELs to apply their growing language abilities to explain events and relationships between events and to integrate and discuss information they have learned from multiple texts on the same topic.

Several common themes resonate throughout the chapters in this volume. One is that young ELs need many social experiences where they interact meaningfully with rich texts, engaging content, and their peers to develop conceptual understandings. At the same time, they need to develop an awareness of how language works to make meaning so that they can draw upon this language awareness as they continue to interpret texts, engage in academic tasks, and produce texts of their own (Derewianka & Jones, 2012). The metaphorical term "scaffolding" (Bruner, 1983; Gibbons, 2009; Vygotsky, 1978a) is also a common thread running throughout these chapters. The authors in each of these chapters demonstrate how ELs are able to engage in cognitively demanding, intellectually rich tasks using complex texts when they are provided with appropriate levels of scaffolding. The examples of scaffolding presented in these chapters illustrate how *temporary* support is adjusted to ELs' particular learning needs in order to improve their access to meaning. As Hammond (2006) has indicated, scaffolding "does not just spontaneously occur" (p. 271). Teachers must know their students well, understand the cognitive and linguistic demands of texts and tasks, plan in advance, and be purposeful about the approaches they use in order for scaffolding to be appropriate for learners' needs.

Several other themes weave these chapters together. One is that attention to second language learning is integrated with attention to content knowledge learning and not addressed in isolation. Whereas teachers need to focus on specific aspects of language (e.g., vocabulary, syntax, text structure and organization) their ELs need to develop in order to be successful in school, this does not mean that language learning should be divorced from content. In fact, the opposite is true. Language and content are inextricably linked (Schleppegrell, 2004). In order for students to learn academic English, they must learn it in the context of intellectually engaging tasks where they interact meaningfully with rich texts and with others and use language to make meaning.

A critical theme that emerges throughout these chapters is that texts and tasks matter. English learners cannot develop academic English if the texts they interact with are simplified and devoid of the rich language they are expected to develop. Tasks matter, too. When students engage in meaningful collaborative conversations about content and about language, they develop new understandings together that they may not have come to on their own. Learning and language are social processes. Teachers can teach some things explicitly, but many understandings need to be developed through meaningful interactions with others. Collaborative conversations that involve extended discourse about rich topics stretch children's thinking and language as they shape and reshape their ideas and the ways they express themselves.

As you will find in the chapters in this volume, ELs in Kindergarten through the fifth grade are in a better position to meet the high expectations of the CCSS for ELA/Literacy and to develop advanced levels of English when they are engaged with intellectually rich and engaging tasks and when their teachers are purposeful about the ways in which they build their students' awareness of how English works to make meaning. When young ELs come to see language as a resource for making meaning and have the linguistic tools to construct these meanings in a variety of contexts, the possibilities are endless.

CHAPTER

2

Interactive Readaloud: A Powerful Technique for Young ELLs

Kristin Lems, National Louis University

Samar Abousalem, Dorn Elementary, Chicago, Illinois

The advent of the Common Core State Standards for English Language Arts and Literacy in History/ Social Studies, Science, and Technical Subjects (CCSS for ELA/Literacy; National Governors Association Center for Best Practices & Council of Chief State School Officers, 2010) has given oral language (the listening and speaking skills) a more prominent role than previously enjoyed in state and national learning standards. That presents both a challenge and an opportunity for planning instruction for ELLs. With the CCSS for ELA/Literacy, speaking and listening have explicit standards of their own; their importance is stated within the standards initiative document:

> To build a foundation for college and career readiness, students *must have ample opportunities to take part in a variety of rich, structured conversations* [emphasis added]—as part of a whole class, in small groups, and with a partner. Being productive members of these conversations requires that students contribute accurate, relevant information; respond to and develop what others have said; make comparisons and contrasts; and analyze and synthesize a multitude of ideas in various domains. (p. 22)

ELLs need to develop both their oral skills and their literacy skills in order to be successful. For ELLs, the powerful relationship between oral language development and literacy is well known (Lems, Miller, & Soro, 2010). The emphasis in the CCSS for ELA/Literacy on oral language development corresponds to a key research finding from studies of successful ESL programs: *instructional conversation*, engaging in goal-directed conversation on an academic topic between a teacher and a small group of students, is consistently found in ESL programs whose students achieved high proficiency levels (Doherty, Hilberg, Pinal, & Tharp, 2003; Saunders & Goldenberg, 1999; Tharp et al., 2003). The recognition that instructional conversation is an important part of the language development process has achieved more prominence for all students and heightened attention in program planning for ELLs (e.g., Doherty et al., 2003; Teemant & Hausman, 2013).

Oral language is represented in multiple CCSS for ELA/Literacy, including at the kindergarten and first-grade levels, and that is a good thing for ELLs. However, educators working with ELLs need to take care to attend to not only the *content demands* of grade-level activities that occur in the early elementary classroom but also the specific *linguistic demands* needed to get the content demands across. This is where teachers of ELLs need to do extra planning in using the CCSS for ELA/Literacy, because the linguistic features of a content task may sometimes be hidden.

Interactive Readaloud: The Rationale

Sometimes referred to as storybook readaloud, story reading, or reading aloud, Interactive Readaloud (IR) consists of expressively reading a book (usually a picture book) aloud to children and stopping at points along the way to engage in dialog about different aspects of the story. This teacher-led activity provides students with a venue in which to actively engage in instructional conversation about a text's title, illustrations, characters, setting, plot, themes, genre, and use of language. At the same time, IR gives children an opportunity to respond emotionally to events, characters, and descriptions found in a text and to relate them to their own lives.

IR gives children in the early elementary years a chance to practice text analysis with the support of a teacher but without the struggles of decoding. Its positive effects are well documented for all students (e.g., Dickinson & Smith, 1994; Elley, 1989; Justice, Meier, & Walpole, 2005; McGee & Schickedanz, 2007; Robbins & Ehri, 1994) and for ELLs in particular (e.g., Collins, 2005; Elley & Mangubai, 1983; Silverman, 2007).

IR also exposes ELLs to themes, settings, and new vocabulary words, helping to build background knowledge and knowledge about how things in the world work. For example, the book we chose for our model lesson, *If You Take a Mouse to School* (Numeroff, 2002), provides considerable information about what happens during a typical school day in America, which is very important for helping young ELLs understand what they are expected to be able to do in school. Finally, ELLs gain language through interaction; research confirms that for ELLs, "beginning reading instruction should emphasize an interactive approach" (Garcia & Bauer, 2004, p. 168).

Not surprisingly, IR addresses several of the CCSS for ELA/Literacy skills, particularly in the reading standards for literature (RL), for kindergarten (K), and first grade (1):

- actively engage in group reading activities with purpose and understanding (RL.K.10)

- ask and answer questions about key details in text (RL.K.1, RL.1.1)

- retell stories including key details (RL.K.2, RL.1.2)

- describe the relationships between the illustrations and the meanings in a story (RL.K.7, RL.1.7)

- recognize common types of texts (RL.K.5, RL.1.5)

- ask and answer questions about unknown words (RL.K.4)

For all of these reasons, IR is an excellent choice for the early elementary ESL classroom.

It's important that teachers take the time to choose the appropriate books for IR and to prepare rich lessons to accompany them, as this overview reminds us (McGee & Schickedanz, 2007):

> The repeated interactive read-aloud approach requires that teachers study closely each book they read. They must craft effective comments and questions and be able to respond on the spot to children's answers, which often indicate misinterpretations and misunderstandings . . . . it is critical that teachers use these strategies so that children engage in analytical thinking. (p. 750)

The following section is a systematic description of a 3-day lesson plan using IR with first-grade ELLs.

Interactive Readaloud Lesson Plan

This 3-day lesson plan is used by one of our two authors, kindergarten and first-grade ESL teacher Samar Abousalem. Samar has chosen the model text *If You Take a Mouse to School* by Laura Numeroff (2002), illustrated by Felicia Bond, using the content demand of *identifying the sequence of events in a story*, and the linguistic demand of *using sequencing words to retell a series of events*. (Because Samar cites individual pages of the book, it will be helpful to readers if they have the book on hand.) A summary of the 3 days of activities appears in Figure 1.

For the next sections, Samar explains how she engages her students in the IR, using this 3-day plan.

First Day: 25–30 Minutes

I always start off the first day's IR activities by inviting the students to the carpet area, allowing them to get comfortable, and engaging in a conversation that will help prepare them for the reading selection. During this conversation piece, I start by sharing an anecdote or asking questions that the students can relate to. For this particular story, I start by asking students what they did this morning before coming to school. As students share their responses about their morning routine, we move into discussing what we usually do at school. Through this conversational warm up, I know that students can relate to the events in the story, from getting ready for school in the morning to the actual flow of a typical school day. I will revisit the students' responses at the end of the lesson to help make connections to the story.

The warm-up activity not only gets the students' attention, but also gives a concrete experience that they can easily connect to and refer back to throughout the lesson. In addition, with this activity, I have also given students the opportunity to talk and listen to their peers in a nonthreatening environment in which no one fears having the wrong answer.

Next, I introduce the cover of the book and tell the students that we will be reading a story about a boy and his mouse and that we will be reading to find out what exciting things happen at school. I have the students identify what they see on the front cover and think about what might happen in the story. Students turn to a partner and share their predictions.

First day, 25–30 minutes	
Before reading	**During reading**
— Activate prior knowledge through teacher anecdote and children relating their daily routines — Make predictions based on cover art — Learn name of author, illustrator, and genre — Highlight key vocabulary words on illustrated sentence strips, define them, and put in pocket chart — Share Read to Find Out Question on chart paper — Share the *content demand* focus—telling story in order — Share the *linguistic demand* focus—sequencing terms — Picture-walk through the book, as students make predictions based on prior knowledge — During picture walk, stop to ask "five W" questions	— Read expressively, stopping at specific points for thinkalouds that address strategy, skill, and Read to Find Out Question — Confirm answers to "five W" questions — Engage students in "think pair share" with a partner at several points to make personal connections to story — Confirm or change predictions made during picture walk as those points come up in book — Write sequencing words and events on chart paper — Revisit Read to Find Out Question — Have students retell the story using sequencing words — Compare mouse's day to students' own school day in whole group
Second day, 25–30 minutes	
Before reading	**During reading**
— Set a purpose for reading—explain that rereading is a powerful strategy — Orally review yesterday's experience with story, looking at chart paper for linguistic demand and pocket chart for vocabulary — Have children retell the story, using sequencing words — Go back to title page, author, genre, and picture walk, asking more inferential questions	— Reread the selection — Model inferencing for unknown vocabulary such as *locker* and *experiment*, through both picture clues and context — Have students complete sentence frames using *build* and *clay* with a partner and then with whole group — Have students draw pictures of how they think the boy feels, share their pictures with a partner and with the class, drawing on personal experiences
Third day, 20–25 minutes	
Before reading	**During reading**
— Have students retell the story using more detail — Have the whole class practice reading sight words that appear in the book (e.g., *his, take, get, then, when, need, want, some, little*) — Pass out specific sight words to individual students; have students listen for them as they occur in the story and respond when theirs comes up — Repeat once more the author, title, and genre of the story	— Model expressive reading while "echo reading" the book with students for several pages — Have students answer more finely grained questions including comparatives or classifications in the book — Have students retell the story using correct sequencing, placing the sequence words in a pocket chart — Have students sort picture cards of the events in the story into the correct order — Move into guided reading with a text on a related topic

Figure 1. Three-Day Lesson Plan Using Interactive Readaloud With First-Grade ELLs

I do a lot of "think pair share" in my classroom because it helps support ELLs' listening and speaking skills so much. These oral skills are now not only part of the WIDA (World-Class Instructional Design and Assessment) standards (WIDA, 2014) but also a CCSS expectation for all students.

Next, I read the book title and names of the author and illustrator, and I ask the students to identify who they are and what role they each have in telling the story (RL.K.6, RL.1.6). I then identify the genre (fantasy) and provide students with a definition of fantasy (RL.K.5, RL.1.5).

At this point, I preteach a few vocabulary words they need to know prior to reading the story. For this book, I focus on the words *build*, *tuck*, and *clay*. I prepare the words on sentence strips and add images to the sentence strips to provide visual support that gives ELLs fuller access to the word. The words are placed in a pocket chart for students to see and refer back to. I choose vocabulary words that students may not know and need to know to understand the text. I find that these are often short, high-frequency words not of Latin origin, words for which students from Hispanic backgrounds do not have a cognate, such as *tuck*. In addition, I also try to pick words that I can utilize outside the readaloud, later in the day. *Build* and *clay* are great examples of such words. *Clay* can be used for a hands-on activity to *build* three dimensional shapes in math, or when we make letters to *build* words. It is important for students to have multiple experiences with the vocabulary words; they should not be taught exclusively within the text, but through it, increasing students' word bank.

Setting a purpose for our reading is very important to provide ELLs with a sense of meaning and focus for the selection (RL.K.10), so at this point, I provide a Read to Find Out Question. For this book, it is: *What exciting things happen when the boy takes his mouse to school?* I have prepared the question on chart paper and posted it on the easel. I also identify the content demand focus (comprehension skill) we will be focusing on, which is identifying the sequence of events. I explicitly define it as "the order that events happen in a story." Further, I inform the students that the linguistic demand focus (strategy) we will be working on is using sequence words to put events in order, which I define as "using your own words to tell the important parts of a story in the order it happens." I post two mini-charts for these, along with the question, to serve as reminders of what we are doing as readers that will help us answer the Read to Find Out Question.

As I do a picture walk through the first few pages of the book, I discuss the things they see on the pages. I try to focus on asking questions that relate to *who, what, when, where, why,* and the prediction question, *How do you think the story will end?* This gets the students engaged in the selection and piques their curiosity. I do not confirm their predictions at that time. For example,

Page 5: (the mouse is putting on his overalls), "What do you think is happening here?" The students will most likely say that the mouse looks like he is getting dressed. "Why do you think he is getting dressed?" Some students might reason that he is going to school because of the book title or because they see the mouse's backpack.

Page 7: (the mouse in the lunchbox), "What do you think the mouse is doing in the lunchbox?" Some responses may be that he is hiding, playing, or looking for food, and this creates enjoyable, imaginative speculation because the mouse can fit in a lunchbox.

Page 13: (working on science experiment), "What is happening in this picture? What do you think will happen next?" Students usually have a variety of answers, such as making a mess, having fun, or mixing something.

Pages 28–29: (mouse playing and crying near the end of the book), "Let's look at these pictures. What do you see? How do you think the mouse feels? Here I can see the mouse looks like he is having fun. Yet on this page he looks like he is upset. Why do you think he looks sad?" Students might say he is tired, or because he has dirty clothes now (RL.1.4).

These are the kinds of questions I want my students to try to answer before I begin to read. I do this in order to help their prediction skills, something I want them to be capable of doing in every book they read. Finally, I ask, "How do you think this story will end?" Students will share this last prediction with their partner. I always stop before the last page or two so as not to give away the ending during the picture walk. A picture walk, turning the pages of the book and talking about the illustrations, allows students the opportunity to preview a story prior to reading it and to start to organize their thoughts about the character, setting, and what they think is happening, before having to focus on listening to the story.

At this point, I tell the students how excited I am to read the story from the beginning to see what really happens. I make sure to read with animation and expression because I can see it helps ELLs further comprehend the story and encourages their active listening. Students demonstrate their active listening to me in a variety of ways, from leaning forward and focusing on the book to making comments and connections. They provide instant feedback that reveals that they are paying attention to and are excited about what they are about to hear. And then I begin to read.

When I arrive at page 5 (the boy is helping the mouse get ready for school), before I start to read, I do a think aloud to incorporate the word *first* to help prepare students to learn the linguistic demands of identifying the sequence of events. "*First*, I see the boy combing the mouse's hair while the mouse puts on his overalls. I see a refrigerator and a sink. The mouse and the boy must be at home. The mouse is getting dressed, so he must be going somewhere. I see some pencils, an eraser, and a small backpack. These are all school supplies. I think he might be going to school."

As I continue to read, I ask one or two students to share their predictions made earlier during the picture walk, and then we compare and confirm or disprove them as we arrive at the appropriate page. I make sure to continue to model sequencing words when the mouse arrives at school. On page 15, I ask, "First the mouse read, next he did some math, then he did some spelling and science, and now he is all clean; what do you think he will do now?" At this point, I try to solicit personal connections to students' own school day and to lunchtime.

On the next couple of pages, we encounter our new vocabulary words and review their meaning in the context of the story (RL.K.4).

On page 23, I ask them, "Where do you think the mouse, the boy, and his classmates are going? Why do you say that?" I want students to notice that the kids have their backpacks and to infer that they only wear their backpacks when they are going home and not to recess (RL.K.2, RL.1.2).

I continue to read and note that the mouse looks like he is having fun, up until page 29. This is the last prediction. I have students turn to their partners and share their earlier responses from the picture walk or change their response. I have a few students share their predictions with the whole class and explain their reasoning. We read the final pages and confirm our prior predictions or modify them.

After we are done reading the story, in order to further address the content and linguistic demands, I ask students to share the events using the sequencing words *first, next, then,* and *last* to help us answer the Read to Find Out Question. I have already printed out images of some of the events, and as the students verbalize the order in which the events happened, I put the events up in order onto the chart paper. Finally, we revisit the Read to Find Out Question and confirm that we were able to identify and answer what exciting things happened when the boy took his mouse to school (RL.K.1, RL.1.1). In concluding the first day's lesson, I ask the students how the mouse's day compares to their day, thereby revisiting our initial conversation (RL.K.2, RL.1.2).

Second Day: 25–30 Minutes

As students gather on the carpet, I engage them in conversation about the book again. I inform them that the book was so much fun to read the first time that we will read it again. It is important for ELLs to understand that rereading is important and that all good readers read a book several times to enjoy it and better comprehend it.

With the book displayed along with the chart, pictures, and vocabulary words posted from the previous lesson, I ask students to retell the story in their own words. Again, I remind them to use *first, next, then,* and *last* as their sentence starters while describing the events. This not only helps them retell the story, but it also promotes correct English sentence structure, a skill most ELLs need to develop.

As with the first day, we start with the discussion of the cover. I read the title and the names of the author and illustrator, asking "Who can tell me what the author does?" "Now, who can tell me what the illustrator does?" (RL.K.6, RL.1.6). I ask about the genre and how students can identify it from the cover (RL.K.5, RL.1.5), and I ask additional questions related to the genre: "Can anyone remember who the characters in the story are?" Moving on to read the title page, I go through and identify everything I see on that page, therefore giving students more vocabulary words. I ask if they can identify what is on the boy's pajamas (chocolate chip cookies) and also ask the students if they can identify what room they are in (bathroom) and how they know for sure (most students will say that they brush their teeth in a bathroom).

Next, on page 6, I model making an inference by doing a think aloud: "I see a jar of peanut butter, jelly, bread, chocolate chip cookies, and a lunchbox. The author did not tell me what the boy is going to make for lunch, but using what I know and clues from the pictures on the page, I think he is going to take a peanut butter and jelly sandwich to school." As I read page 10, I ask questions about the word *locker,* which we do not have in our school, and use rereading to see if they can figure out its meaning through visual context clues. I then have students share with a partner what they think a locker is, and why. I repeat the procedure with the word *experiment* on page 13. While these words may be more difficult for ELLs in the early primary grades, especially in isolation, the visual representation along with expressive reading make them easily accessible. That is an important reason why IRs are so important for ELLs.

Reading on to pages 16, 17, and 18, we encounter the vocabulary words *build* and *clay* from the first lesson. Here, after I read each page, I ask the students to think of something they would like to *build* using the sentence frame "I would like to build _____ with _____" and share it with a partner. I go through the class and have one partner share what the other wanted to build. I do the same thing with the word *clay*, using the sentence frame "I can use clay to make _____" and now ask the other partner to share. This gives all the students an opportunity to listen and speak in a small group and then in a larger group, further increasing ELLs' speaking, listening, and vocabulary practice. With these two vocabulary words and the sentence frame, many students are able to make connections to creating three-dimensional shapes in math class, and therefore, academic words such as *sphere*, *cylinder*, and *cube* are used to complete the sentence frame.

Moving forward in the book, as I finish reading page 22, I review the meaning of *tuck* and ask students why they think the character "tucked" the book in a safe place. Students usually can infer that the book is important and that he doesn't want anyone to take it or lose it.

At the conclusion of the story, I ask the students how they think the mouse felt at the end of the book and to explain their reasoning (RL.1.4). Their response is usually that he was happy because he can be seen eating his snack and smiling. This time, because there is no picture of the boy at the end of the story, I have them think about how the boy might have felt. I have them go back to their seats to draw a picture to illustrate how the boy feels. I divide the class into three groups, have each group share their pictures and discuss how they think the boy felt at the end of the story, and explain their reasoning. Here, students can further demonstrate listening and speaking skills, engage in instructional conversation, and infer how the boy feels based on their own personal experiences or opinions. Finally, I have the students retell the story, using a lot of details to describe each event in addition to sequencing terms (RL.K.1–3, RL1.1–3).

Third Day: 20–25 Minutes

As students gather on the carpet, I engage them in conversation about the book. With the book displayed along with the chart, pictures, and vocabulary words posted from the previous lessons, I ask students to retell the story in their own words. However, this time I don't prompt them along as much as in the previous lessons, and I expect and encourage them to add as many details of the story as possible (RL.K.7, RL.1.7). We review the title, author, and illustrator and their roles in the story (RL.K.6, RL.1.6). Before we continue to read, we review sight words as a whole group. I provide each student with a sight word written on a card and a piece of highlighter tape. Students are usually very excited to do this part because they enjoy going up to the book and highlighting "their word" as we read the story. Moving forward, I invite the students to echo read (repeat what I read) a few pages with me. This helps students acquire expressive language. After reading several pages, I pause to elicit higher level thinking from the students. For example, as I read this time, I mention how the students are always focused on what the mouse is doing and ask them to use the pictures to help them figure out why. This time, I am not looking for simple answers such as seeing a mouse in school, but noticing that everything the mouse does is bigger and more difficult than what is normally done in their class (they realize this by looking at the students' math equations and spelling words).

Once we get to the mouse eating his lunch, I model thinking out loud and questioning what kind of sandwich it might be. Again, I have students share their response with a partner and call on a few students to share their response and reasoning. For example, a student might say, "It is peanut butter because it looks brown," and another student might recall the illustration of the boy making his own lunch beside a jar of peanut butter and jelly. Finally, as we finish up the story, I have students retell the story again, identifying the sequence of events and using sequencing words (RL.K.7, RL.1.7). I call on students to sort picture cards of the events into the correct order, using correct sequencing terms as they arrange the story in a pocket chart. I wrap up the lesson by sharing how much I loved this story and how it is a favorite of mine.

To further build onto the IR experience, I always tie the story into my guided reading selection, which supports the small-group component of instructional conversation. In both kindergarten and first grade, I conduct guided reading.

In guided reading, students are divided into small reading groups of four to five students, based on their English reading proficiency or level. During guided reading, students read a different story page by page, as a group. Students then answer comprehension questions for each page and discuss words they struggled with or strategies they used to help them understand word meanings. After the students have read the guided reading selection at least twice, I have them compare the characters and setting to those of our IR selection (RL.K.9–10, RL.1.9–10). Then we compare and contrast the events from both selections. It is during this phase that I also appreciate how much my students have learned from the IR. Students generally display confidence in speaking and making comparisons about the readaloud story.

Choosing the Book and Planning the Lesson

A lot of thought goes into choosing the book that will be used for an IR. While the book should be enjoyable for students and pertain to an area that interests them, it must also be a purposeful reading selection. For starters, I want the book to have rich pictures or photographs to draw my students in. These images can be used to build more descriptive sentences or ask questions that pertain to the details in the images, further increasing students' listening and speaking skills. Another element in the book that I am looking for is rich vocabulary. I want the book to offer several opportunities to introduce new words for the students to learn or words that have multiple meanings. Finally, I want the reading selection to lend itself to many teaching opportunities. For many good suggestions for using IR and obtaining suitable IR books, please consult the work of Jim Trelease (2013, 2014) for both books and online resources.

When selecting the specific book for an IR, I also pay great attention to a variety of criteria, such as:

- making sure a variety of genres is read to my students (exposing students to different genres is imperative for ELLs, especially now with the call for more informational text in CCSS);

- making sure that the IR ties into the theme of the reading series I'm using;

- providing students with an opportunity to engage with multiple books by the same author (author study);

- finding a reading selection that my ELLs can relate to the book at some point in the story; and

- making sure the book builds background knowledge for my ELLs.

For the last criterion, I appreciate that the book chosen for this chapter builds knowledge around the sequence of events that occur in the day of a typical American student. The book helps build familiarity with the school structure and culture and can be directly applied to the students' expectations of experiences inside and outside of the classroom.

In preparing for the lesson, I usually go through the entire book and mark it with Post-it notes. I identify the vocabulary words that I want to focus on and define. I also use the Post-it notes to identify the questions I want to ask on each page as well as where I want to model a think aloud. Doing this in advance of teaching the lesson helps me make sure that the lesson flows from one day to the next while scaffolding students' comprehension skills and increasing their listening and speaking skills.

Here are some of the specific strategies that I use for my ELLs during an IR:

- posting the vocabulary words with pictures, Read to Find Out Questions, and mini-charts of the strategy and skill;

- providing students with turn and share, as well as whole group, opportunities to help support listening and speaking skills;

- providing sentence frames to help support language acquisition and oral language proficiency; and

- providing opportunities to read the text multiple times to help support and enhance students' reading comprehension.

Challenges in Using IR With ELLs

One challenge that is easy to encounter when using IRs with ELLs is difficulty maintaining students' interest for very long on the third day. They sometimes feel they've answered all the questions they want to answer. For this reason, I caution against spending too much time asking questions. Ask fewer questions, yet strive for questions that require higher level thinking.

However, therein lies another challenge: finding higher level questions that will elicit answers that the students are able to produce. The best solution for this is a well thought out lesson plan so that the two previous days leading up to the third day set the foundation for making deeper connections and inferences.

Extensions and Concluding Thoughts

IR is most often associated with story books at the K–2 level, but there are many possibilities for using it with older students and with informational texts. The text might come from the daily newspaper, or a science or geography book, or from something found on the Internet. When it comes from the Internet, there might be accompanying images that can be shown on a whiteboard so that there is a visual feature to accompany the oral reading.

IR can also be performed by readers other than the teacher. These might include guest authors, student readers from higher grades at the school or from a partner school, parent volunteers, or even members of the class who practice a reading in advance. Stories can also be found in podcasts and video streams on the Internet, some read by well-known actors or entertainers, but in that case, the interactive piece is removed, and along with it, a great deal of the benefit.

As Samar's sample lesson indicates, written words can be included to guide teachers to address the content and linguistic demands of the instructional unit, as long as they do not overwhelm the oral nature of the activity. It is even possible to combine the technique with drawing activities, such as the one Samar described, or writing activities, such as quick writes that respond to some of the teacher's questions. An especially good question for predicting is "What do you think will happen next?" Some questions can even serve as a writing prompt, such as the question, "What would you do if this happened to you?" The written responses can then be shared with a partner.

There are few early literacy techniques that touch upon more of the CCSS for ELA/Literacy while also employing best practices for ELLs than Interactive Readaloud. It is through IR that the teacher and students not only share the book, but truly experience it. Engaging interactions between the teacher and the students bring the book, its characters, plot, and content to life in the classroom. Children not only develop listening and speaking skills and new vocabulary, but take part in an adventure the class can embark upon every day.

Reflection Questions and Action Plans

1. Think of several books you use in the classroom and evaluate whether these might be good candidates for IR. Do they meet the criteria described by Samar? In your experience, are there additional factors that might make a book a good candidate for an IR?

2. When you are preparing questions for your readaloud for students to discuss and think about, how do you make sure to include not just factual questions, but also open-ended questions that require a more extensive, thoughtful response? With careful planning, these can be included even if the students are at a beginning or entering proficiency level of English. Samar talked about the delicate balance of constructing deeper questions while making sure students are able to answer at their current proficiency level. How do you find that balance?

3. How do you address the need for greater wait time for ELLs that are just beginning to say their first few words or phrases in English? What kind of system of supports might you set up to gently deter more orally fluent children from automatically jumping in?

4. How does your vocal intonation and expressive reading help convey meaning in your oral reading? How would you advise that new teachers or teacher candidates develop this skill?

Action Plan

Choose an IR book you think is a good choice and create a 3-day lesson plan that parallels the one in this chapter. In addition to writing the questions and choosing the stopping points for the story, you will need to

- create the cards with the target vocabulary words,

- choose the Read to Find Out Question that will inform the whole activity and write it on a large readable sign, and

- choose the strategy and skill that will be the focus of the IR.

Most schools will provide a lesson plan format that includes the CCSS for ELA/Literacy, so it will be necessary to identify and match them while developing the lessons. When teachers try the unit out for the first time, they should take care to jot down notes to see what worked well and what needs a little "tweaking" for the next time around. To organize sets of IR lessons, one might use a tote box with hanging files to store the lesson plans along with the books and other materials. As the set grows, it will get easier, and, finally one day, you may find that you have become not only proficient in IR, but the school's resident expert. You will also have the greatest satisfaction of all: sharing a reading experience with eager young learners.

Scaffolding Academic Literacy in a Science Inquiry Project

Barbara Merino, Michele Fortes, Laura Dubcovsky, and Joanne Galli-Banducci
University of California, Davis

Scaffolding: a teaching style that supports and facilitates the student as he or she learns a new skill or concept, with the ultimate goal of the student becoming self-reliant. Derived from the theories of Russian psychologist Lev Vygotsky (1896–1934), in practice it involves teaching material just beyond the level at which the student could learn alone. (American Psychological Association, 2009, p. 364)

How might insights from teacher research inform how teachers can scaffold instruction designed to address Common Core State Standards (CCSS) with ELs? We have chosen to focus on scaffolding because it is one of the most widely endorsed instructional practices for ELs and because it offers substantive benefits for instruction in linguistically and culturally diverse classrooms. Despite the multiple advantages of scaffolding, this approach is often elusive and misunderstood (Wells, 1996; Van de Pol, Volman, & Beishuizen, 2010). The principal challenges to effectively implementing scaffolding include (a) applying generic strategies without exploring whether the strategy meets the demands of the concepts or tasks; (b) differentiating the scaffolds in response to evolving EL needs; (c) understanding the cognitive, linguistic, and cultural features to consider in designing the scaffolds.

In this chapter, we share insights on scaffolding academic literacy from exemplary beginning teacher research at the elementary level. We draw from our experiences as teacher educators mentoring teachers doing research case studies in culturally and linguistically diverse communities (Merino & Dixon, 2010). We present illustrative practices informed by the research, guiding teachers' development and the data gathering that shaped the exploration on how to develop targeted concepts and language skills. We discuss these practices through one elaborated case, Rosa, a Latina bilingual certified teacher working in a second/third-grade combination class in a rural setting, in a K–8 school, with 52% ELs. To develop her students' descriptive skills, Rosa used project-based learning in a short inquiry project on snails. Rosa selected project-based learning for her study in part because of her own experiences studying snails. Moreover, animal study projects have often been successfully implemented with young children, and many examples appear in the professional literature. These studies include Possick's (2007) research on kindergarteners' study of a pet rabbit, and McGough and Nyberg's (2013) research on second graders' study of habitats with multiple animals.

We define teacher research as systematic investigations of how teaching influences student learning over time in a single classroom or learning community. This inquiry is intentional, contextual, ethical, and, above all, responsive to the learners' strengths and challenges. We believe teacher research is most productive in culturally and linguistically diverse settings when it is informed through a framework of social justice and educational equity (Cochran-Smith, 2004). Finally, we have found that teacher research focused on ELs can provide teachers with leverage in understanding student development and enable even beginning teachers to design or adapt instruction through data-driven decision making (Merino & Ambrose, 2009). Here we will provide an illustration of how teacher research enabled Rosa to target science, a subject not taught in her school, as a way to develop literacy.

The Standards

The Common Core State Standards, adopted by 45 states in the United States, have been defined as "a progression of learning expectations" in English language arts and mathematics "designed to prepare K–12 students to be career and college ready" (Roskos & Neuman, 2013, p. 469). Standards have been evolving rapidly in California, particularly with the adoption of the Common Core State Standards for English Language Arts and Literacy in History/Social Studies, Science, and Technical Subjects (CCSS for ELA/Literacy; National Governors Association Center for Best Practices & Council of Chief State School Officers, 2010). Few scholars have focused on the challenges and opportunities these standards present to ELs (Lee, Quinn, & Valdes, 2013).

In the teacher research studies we mentor, each teacher researcher (TR) is asked to identify a set of standards that apply to the learning domain targeted and to justify how the standards would support learning. After exploring the perspectives of their context and gathering preliminary data on their students, TRs identify a concept to develop and explore relevant research and professional literature to design data collection procedures to track development. TRs then develop a multiweek instructional cycle responsive to their students' needs, drawing on a short review of the research literature to shape their projects. TRs must consult teacher research case studies, the professional literature for the area of the curriculum targeted, scholarly reviews of multiple studies, and at least one quasi-experimental study or qualitative study targeting some aspect of their lesson study.

Rosa teaches in a rural school largely serving children of farm workers. She teaches a second/third-grade combination classroom, with 16 students—10 second graders and 6 third graders—of which 10 are ELs, most at intermediate or early advanced levels with the lowest scores in writing as measured by California English Language Development Test (CELDT) used for EL identification. There is high mobility in the class, reflecting the seasonal farm labor opportunities available to parents. Most students ($N=12$) attended all sessions.

The CCSS Writing Standards and Rosa's Lesson Study

For her master's project, Rosa wanted to explore writing for authentic purposes while integrating other modalities: speaking, listening, and reading. She decided to focus on an inquiry approach to learning through a lesson cycle, targeting observation in science with an investigation about snails. See Table 1 for an outline of the specific CCSS for ELA/Literacy that apply to Rosa's case of second/third grade in writing.

Table 1. CCSS for ELA/Literacy Targeted in Rosa's Lesson Cycle

CCSS Standard	Focus and Rosa's Data Sources	Contextual Features	Task/Text Features; Language and Content Demands
Writing—Grade 2			
#4	Production and distribution of writing *Baseline/outcome descriptions of snails*	With guidance and support from adults *Photos/live snails observations*	Produce writing in which the development and organization are appropriate to task and purpose Language—Vocabulary for color, shape, body features Content—Criteria for a scientific description based on observation
# 7	Research to build/present knowledge *KWL on class snail knowledge*	Participate in shared research and writing projects . . . to build and present knowledge	Text types appropriate to the grade—informative/explanatory texts . . . conveying ideas and information clearly
#8	Recall information from experience or gather it *Recalled and direct experience with wild animals*	Prompted with cues, after an experience or gathered from provided resources	Write informative/explanatory texts . . . with the goal of answering a question
#10	Range of writing *Daily entries in science journal*	Write routinely . . . for a range of discipline specific tasks	Variety of tasks across disciplines . . . or a range of tasks, purposes and audiences
Writing—Grades 1–3			
#1	Writing across text types *Daily entries in science journal*	Write to convey information/ideas *Scaffolded questioning*	Examine a topic Convey ideas clearly *How do snails move? What do they eat?*
#2	Writing across text types *Journal entries* *What happened when . . .?*	Write narrative texts of real . . . experiences or events.	Using effective technique . . . descriptive details . . . clear event sequences
#3	Writing across text types *KWL snails*	Conduct short research projects	Build knowledge about a topic *Snail reports; oral/written*

The CSSS for ELA/Literacy writing standards most relevant for Rosa's inquiry in second/third grade included building knowledge and writing different text types, including answering questions. Rosa used the following data sources to explore students' development on the targeted standards:

1. Preliminary data: an individual writing sample about recalled wildlife experiences collected after reading a story about a similar experience

2. A class-generated KWL (what we know, want to know, and have learned) used as an ongoing record about snails as the lesson cycle progressed

3. Baseline and outcome data: individual written descriptions after pairs' observations of snails

4. Daily formative assessment: daily science journal entries on what students learned about snails each day, co-constructed with the teacher

The lead content demands for the science inquiry approach Rosa used include understanding how scientific observations resemble yet are different from everyday observation. Students must learn how to observe with minimal disruption to the snail, and how to represent what is actually in evidence in response to a question (review of the literature—Eberback & Crowley, 2009). The lead language demands for the task of reporting on a structured observation about a snail include not only the vocabulary of snail key features (e.g., the shape and the colors of the shell), but also specific grammatical structures, such as *ongoing present* as a verb tense, to use with descriptions. For ELs, an added demand is making the descriptions rich enough with details to capture size, shape, shell color, and patterns in ways that distinguish one snail from another.

To illustrate how Rosa identified and addressed the language and content demands of assessments, we present one of her data sources. The ELA curriculum Rosa was required to use in her district presents a typical approach for collecting writing samples: asking students to recall an experience similar to what they had read in a story. We will later contrast this elicitation approach with Rosa's more scaffolded technique, where she set up description as linked to observation. The approach guided students through a specific set of questions that prompted discussion and helped ELs especially to co-construct descriptions after a preliminary snail observation. Here is one of Rosa's data sources:

Data source 1: preliminary data

> Rosa's ELA curriculum writing prompt: "Have you ever seen signs of wildlife in the school playground or in your neighborhood? Tell about them."

Sample student response:

> I saw a lizard in the playground. There's sometimes spiders near the door outside. One time an ant bit me. (Andres, Latino; bilingual native English speaker; third grade)

Rosa's analysis, from her inquiry report, targets description and responsiveness to the prompt:

> This sample shows that the student responded to the question with a relevant answer. The student gives details and describes where wildlife was seen; however, the student doesn't use descriptive language when writing about the wildlife.

Writing or discussion prompts such as these may be part of everyday practice, but they may present challenges that are not readily apparent. The content demands of the prompt require understanding of the question in general, first, to call up experiences seeing wildlife defined as "wild animals in their natural environment" (Scholastic Reference, 2002, p. 620). The term *wildlife* might present some challenges to ELs. Though the term was featured in the reading, an example of wildlife would have been helpful in order to scaffold understanding of the prompt. The word *signs* here has a more complex meaning in scientific terms and even in everyday use: "a trace or evidence left by someone" (Scholastic Reference, 2002, p. 490). Students must recall the instances as well as the location of where wildlife was seen, with some details of the setting. This presents another set of cognitive demands. Students not only have to recall what was seen but also where it was seen and the traces of evidence left behind. The final challenge for an EL would be in constructing a cohesive paragraph with sufficient descriptive detail to re-create the event. The most likely response would be a list of animals, with some descriptive details. The response produced above by Andres focused on listing the wildlife seen and where it was seen, closing with a dramatic event, being bitten by an ant. In sum, the cognitive demands of this writing prompt may be challenging for many students, and the language demands of the task are substantive for an EL.

Rosa's analysis seems apt, and, in fact, most students in the class showed a pattern of providing few descriptive details on wildlife. Rosa recognized the limitations of eliciting description without a recent direct experience and an authentic motivation to communicate. Rosa's purpose in conducting her teacher research, as stated in her Teacher Research Plan, was to "improve students' use of descriptive language by integrating science curriculum through a lesson cycle that focuses on student exploration of snails."

In addition to the ELA text prompt, Rosa used other data sources for her study: (a) questions generated by her students in pairs and in a whole-group discussion (captured on a KWL chart) after having a short period of observation of live snails in pairs, and (b) a short written description of a snail (pre/post) to be included in their science notebooks with the date and context noted. These additional data sources were designed expressly to establish a baseline for description, and students' conceptual understanding of snails was strategically linked to guided inquiry about what snails look like in general and how they can differ in color, shape, and size. Comparing these techniques of data collection to the ELA curriculum's prompt to recall a wildlife experience, it is understandable why the snail observations would be more effective. These assessments were more authentic and engaging. Most important, all were effectively scaffolded with multiple supports.

Rosa's questions for her teacher research and lesson study follow:

How does the study of snails targeting observations and descriptions improve students' use of descriptive language in writing?

How does scaffolding descriptive language through targeting snails' key features (size, color, body shape, parts, movement, and anatomy) facilitate students' use of descriptors in their writing?

The genesis of the research question and focus of her instruction as tracked by earlier artifacts from the inquiry classes demonstrate that, from early on, Rosa had been relying on data from her students to make instructional and inquiry decisions. In Rosa's September Context Field Notes, she wrote:

> I was surprised to see the specifics of my students' CELDT scores because three of my ELs have high academic achievement (yet their writing scores are low. . . . I have to get data on the CSTs).

By October, Rosa was committed to targeting writing as the lead construct. Initially, she was interested in pursuing writing conventions. Based on her review of unit assessments on the weekly story in the ELA text, she wondered in her field notes about form and function:

> Do they understand that every sentence needs to start with a capital and end with a punctuation mark? Are they thinking about what they are going to write before they write? Are there patterns in the way they write their sentences? Starting with *because*, for example.

The research literature that supported her instructional approach targeted observation as the linchpin for motivating description, linking talking and writing in mixed-ability groups, the use of pictorials as scaffolds during classroom composing, and a multisensory approach to observation in pairs. Rosa also sought to develop her students' understanding of what it means to observe like scientists.

Rosa outlined her instructional approach as authentic inquiry about snails, scaffolded through guided observation of photographs of snails first, and daily investigations with actual snails over 7 days. The focus on observing and describing what snails look like with particular attention to the color and shape of their shells illustrates the concept of slicing down some aspect of the learning domain that is a good candidate for having the learner work independently. This is an example of identifying what resources are essential for learners as the teacher identifies what learners are likely to be able to do on their own if sufficient scaffolding is provided in the co-constructed stage.

Rosa began with photographs of snails in multiple colors, where the full range of the students' color spectrum knowledge could be activated first. Identifying prior knowledge fulfills two necessary characteristics for an effective scaffold: accessing support from the learners' language resources and suggesting ways these could be adapted to fit the task, that is, more color-accurate descriptions of the snails observed. Like English, Spanish also mixes colors to convey a richer color mix: *verde amarillo* for yellowish green, for example. This strategy helps bilingual students learn how to combine color names to more accurately capture the range of colors in the snails, combining brown and black, for example, as brownish black or brown striped or grey speckled with black. See Figure 1 for an overview of the lesson cycle.

Rationale for the Use of Scaffolding

Scaffolding Definitions and Frameworks

Over the past 30 years, scaffolding of children's learning has been the object of educational research in a variety of contexts. Scaffolding is usually linked to Vygotsky's (1978b) sociocultural theory and the zone of proximal development, characterized as "the distance between the actual developmental level as determined through independent problem solving and the level of potential development as determined through problem solving under adult guidance or in collaboration with more capable

Lesson cycle

- ☐ 7 sessions, 45 minutes each—focus of sessions varied by day
- ☐ Each session included observation time
- ☐ Students wrote in science journal every day at the end of the session
- ☐ Students engaged in authentic inquiry on their own, in groups and as a class

Day 1: Introduce the Unit
- ☐ Class discussion: What are snails? Who has seen a snail? Where? What do we know about snails?
- ☐ Observed images and live snails; *lead scaffold: Photos/live snails
- ☐ Wrote predescriptions; *lead scaffold: Class KWL with observation
- ☐ Home connection: Interview parents about snails

Day 2: Snail Details and Snail Races—How Do Snails Move?
- ☐ Review KWL and observed body parts; *word chart—Ss labels
- ☐ Focused on movement; scaffolded questioning
- ☐ Snail races

Day 3: What Do Snails Eat?
- ☐ Discussed what snails might eat; co-constructed questions; KWL
- ☐ Explored and learned about foods snails eat
- ☐ Observed snails eat lettuce, noting where/how it was consumed

Day 4: Snail Anatomy—What Makes a Snail a Snail?
- ☐ Discussed and explored snail anatomy; KWL update
  - ☐ First, students speculated about the snails' anatomy
  - ☐ Then, teacher directed exploration of snail anatomy
- ☐ Used snail diagram (mouth, +tentacles, +eye spots, +apex, shell, foot, mouth, +respiratory pore); teacher added technical labels (+) to the chart
- ☐ Students measured, drew, and labeled their snails

Day 5: What Is Descriptive Language?
- ☐ Introduced and reviewed descriptive language
- ☐ Co-constructed additions to the word chart of descriptive words
- ☐ Pair share of oral descriptions of snails

Day 6: Describing Snails
- ☐ Reviewed word chart; KWL
- ☐ Observed the snails
- ☐ Snail anatomy assessment—label a drawing
- ☐ Post snail description—without word chart

Day 7: Review and Readaloud
- ☐ Overview of unit key events
- ☐ Read aloud to *The Snail's Spell* by Joanne Ryder (1988)
- ☐ Story allows visualization and snail perspective of the world
- ☐ Free-response to readaloud with lead questions

Figure 1. Overview of Rosa's Instructional Approach—Lesson Cycle

peers" (p.86). To represent its function, scaffolding was first used as a metaphor to convey that it should be used with learners as a temporary support (Wood, Bruner, & Ross, 1976).

In a recent review on scaffolding, van de Pol et al. (2010) addressed the effectiveness of scaffolding and identified three essential characteristics in the conceptualization of scaffolding: contingency, fading, and transfer of responsibility. They proposed a comprehensive conceptual model in which contingency is a key characteristic, often operationalized as responsiveness, or differentiated support. Contingent scaffolds are tailored to learners at their individual level of performance to the degree possible as differentiated support. Fading refers to the need for teachers to reduce the support as students improve their performance. Transfer of responsibility is viewed as an essential step to insure that students move toward independent performance. This view of scaffolding suggests that the teacher must adapt support to fit students' needs on an ongoing basis.

The first essential step then is to engage in a formative assessment, sometimes referred to as dynamic assessment (Swanson & Lussier, 2001) or, less formally, monitoring and checking students' understanding (Garza, 2009). For true scaffolding to be in place, teachers must monitor understanding and engagement across the range of student performance and give specific targeted feedback to improve performance. According to a review of the research on feedback (Hattie & Timperley, 2007), to be effective, teachers' feedback must be responsive to the learners' needs and performance: teachers must outline which aspects of the task were met, indicate aspects of the ultimate goal of the task still not reached, and, most important, indicate where to go next to improve. Hattie and Timperley conceptualized this cycle as requiring three essential moves: feedback, feed up, and feed forward. Feedback should be differentiated based on student needs. Feedback given by the teacher or peers should be specific enough that the learner can use it to adjust performance. Response to feedback can help the teacher adjust the scaffolding, making it *contingent* on the level the student or a group of students needs. Rosa's analysis of student responses informed her adjustments to the word chart, making strategic additions to the co-constructed word chart as one way of making that scaffold a differentiated support.

Fading, or the gradual withdrawal of the scaffolding, is a key but often neglected feature of the scaffolding model (Stone, 1998). The rate of fading will depend on the child's development and proficiency in a particular area. For example, the teacher might fade or decrease the support for reading by reducing the intensity of guided questioning (Echevarria, Vogt, & Short, 2008). Nevertheless, the teacher continues to monitor children's performance during this stage to adjust instruction as necessary. Rosa also monitored engagement on an ongoing basis, usually by using classroom sweeps. For example, she used a simple protocol of "eyes on the page" or "hands with a pencil taking notes" to check for engagement, targeting tables around the room. Rosa also took notes on how "focus" students, selected to represent English skills across the range, performed. These data sources were then used to inform subsequent instruction.

This fading process eventually results in the third characteristic of scaffolding outlined in the model: removal of the scaffold. At this stage, identified as the transfer of responsibility, the learner has taken increasing control. The focus then is not simply in completing the task but in doing so independently of visible scaffolds, because the student might now be relying on metacognitive strategies or has internalized the scaffold (Stone, 1998; Vacca, 2008).

Several suggestions for an integrated framework of scaffolding strategies have been proposed. For example, Tharp and Gallimore (1988) presented six means of assisting performance. Some examples include modeling, feeding back, instructing, questioning, and cognitive structuring. Van de Pol et al. (2010) have integrated these frameworks to sharply distinguish between the intentions, or goals, of scaffolding—what is being scaffolded—from the tools or means, that is, how scaffolding is accomplished. In their framework, they provide five scaffolding intentions and six tools. We report next on how scaffolding goals or "What is being scaffolded?" is discussed in the model with illustrations from Rosa's case, as appropriate. Van de Pol et al. propose three types of scaffolding goals: support of students' (1) metacognitive activities, (2) cognitive activities, and (3) affect. We have added two more support types: (4) support of language resources and (5) support through integration of cultural resources. This integrated framework is illustrated in Table 2.

Scaffolding and Inquiry-Based Science

Scaffolding conceived as a complex framework of strategies is especially effective when ELs are asked to participate in authentic science inquiry. Inquiry-based teaching has been defined in various ways in the science education reform literature (Furtak, Seidel, Iverson, & Briggs, 2012): from adopting "scientific ways of knowing, a way for students to learn science" to "an instructional approach and curriculum materials" (p. 304). Furtak et al. define inquiry-based science teaching in terms of the cognitive and social activities of the students and the guidance provided by their teacher, peers, or curriculum. They emphasize the need to expose students to the methods of discovery, the procedural domain, asking scientifically oriented questions and designing studies, executing the procedures, and representing and analyzing their data, but also communicating their findings while working in groups in which students reason collectively. Inquiry-based science teaching operates on a continuum from teacher-led traditional instruction to teacher-guided inquiry and student-led inquiry or discovery at the other extreme. Rosa's approach included teacher modeling combined with guided opportunities to explore and discuss children's findings particularly focused on the description of the snails.

Scaffolding and Language Learning

Scaffolding may also be viewed from a sociocultural/sociolinguistic perspective to learning (Zuengler & Miller, 2006). Halliday and Martin (1993) argue that whenever we use language there are two kinds of contexts. First, there is the context of culture, defined by a community of speakers, writers, readers, and listeners who share common beliefs and expectations about how to communicate—as scientists, for example. Second, there is the context of situation, the particular situation in which language is used for a particular purpose. The context is shaped by three features: (1) what is being talked about or written, (2) the relationship between the writer/reader or speaker/listener, and (3) whether the language is spoken or written. Halliday and Hasan (1989) label these features as follows: *Field* refers to the topic of the text; *tenor* refers to the relationship between the writer/reader or speaker listener; *mode* refers to the channel of communication: listening, speaking, reading, and writing. These three features play a key role on how communication is shaped. Together these three features constitute what is referred to as the *register* of a text.

In Rosa's case, snails were the topic (field); Rosa took the role of team leader of the inquiry, with the students as novices learning how to observe snails (tenor), listening as she prompted ways of supporting their findings orally first, and in writing later. Rosa relied on multiple modes or channels of communication, using oral channels first and linking these to written ones later. In a fluid process, Rosa relied on active listening with both nonverbal and verbal responses. She asked her students to consult with each other as they made their notes, encouraging them to use Spanish if they needed to. She encouraged communication with parents at home as informants and as an audience for students to share their findings. Because she was working with ELs, she was very

Table 2. Integrated Scaffolding Model

Goals (Intentions) Support of Students'	Goal Focus	Tools and Means	Rosa's Strategy/Research That Affirms Its Use
Metacognitive activities	Direction maintenance	• Modeling • Explaining • Questioning *Example:* Snail study as a project informed by questions	Concept & knowledge maps linked to KWL (Nesbit & Adesope, 2006)
Cognitive activities I	Cognitive structuring	• Feedback • Explaining • Questioning *Example:* Rosa's community of practice	Scientific observation (Eberback & Crowley, 2009)
Cognitive activities II	Reduction of degrees of freedom	• Modeling • Questioning • Explaining *Example:* Rosa's word chart, *Drawing as an aide*	Slicing down tasks—vocabulary (Marulis & Neuman, 2010)
Affect I	Recruitment	• Assisting • Explaining • Questioning • Instructing *Example:* Student scientific teams	Cooperative task structures (Rohrbeck et al., 2003)
Affect II	Contingency management/frustration control	• Feedback • Explaining • Assisting *Example:* Rosa's pair share—feedback to teams on how to improve	Peer-assisted learning and feedback model (Hattie & Timperley, 2007)
Language activities	Identifying and scaffolding language demands	• Modeling • Instructing • Assisting *Example:* Rosa's focus—description as text	Scaffolding language/text in lesson cycles (Gibbons, 2002, 2009)
Cultural resources	Differentiating demands of contexts—culture and situation Supporting with cultural resources	• Assisting • Explaining • Questioning *Example:* Rosa's outreach to parents—use of L1	Culturally relevant pedagogy (Lee, Quinn, & Valdes, 2013)

Source: Adapted from Van de Pol et al. (2010)

careful to mentor students in directed listening, especially as they observed the snail. Reading and writing channels of communication were first presented through modeling, followed by shared co-construction, followed by independent work. This scenario is often characterized as "I do, we do, and you do." Rosa was careful to fade her support for individual students when they understood the task and could then model questions or descriptors for peers.

Instructional Approach and Lead Strategy: Scaffolding

Next, we explore how scaffolding can facilitate the development of academic language through scientific inquiry about animals. Rosa justified her selection of snails as relevant to her students' prior knowledge from living in a rural area, in families of farm workers, and her students' enthusiasm for the topic.

The choice of animal to observe in a classroom is a critical step and here a teacher must be responsive to students' age and maturity as well as the length of the study. One kindergarten teacher, for example, chose a goldfish and earthworms because she wanted animals that her students could take care of over a long period while observing them easily (Plevyak & Arlington, 2012). Rosa knew she could collect snails from her garden and that she could also get her students to bring snails to school. Rosa also wanted to focus on just one animal species that would offer the opportunity to experience wide variation in size and age. The selection of one species also fosters close observation of key features to distinguish one animal from another.

Rosa saw that she needed to design scaffolds that would help her to promote inquiry by exploring scientific questions through observation but that would also support the development of descriptive language. To scaffold the observation phase, she provided live snails to observe, materials to draw with, and a protocol for note taking. Rosa was not in a designated bilingual classroom, but all of her students had bilingual skills. She used Spanish strategically to underscore key ideas and to support the ELs when she perceived misunderstandings or when she saw opportunities to apply language knowledge from Spanish that could pertain to English (Marulis & Neuman, 2010; Lee et al., 2013).

Rosa first led an interactive discussion with the children on focus questions, first presenting them as a bilingual list. This strategic use of Spanish to complement and underscore the lead goals of the snail study facilitated her students' sharing with their parents in multiple home–school connections later.

She and her students co-constructed a word wall/chart, organized by the features aligned with their inquiry: size, color, body parts, movement, and shape. Rosa enhanced the opportunities to develop descriptive language by setting up multiple meaningful observations over 7 days as part of a co-constructed exploration of snails. Each session lasted 45 minutes and targeted a different focus every day using a guiding question for the day's inquiry. The KWL guided the discussion of the first day. This was framed globally: What do we want to learn about snails?

KWLs are widely used to begin science explorations with children as a type of group concept map (Nesbit & Adesope, 2006). Possick (2007), for example, used this scaffold on a study of a pet rabbit she brought to her kindergartners. By posing questions about what children know and what they want to know, children gain more ownership of their inquiry. Questions generated can then be clustered in two groups: questions that are researchable via observation and those which would require interviewing an expert or reading an informative text. This approach helps students define what is observable. Students can then develop an understanding of scientific observation of animals as inquiry (Folsom, Hunt, Cavicchio, Schoenemann, & D'Amatao, 2007). The context, the time, and the conditions of the observation are noted, and the animals' responses to stimuli, a spray of water for a snail, for example, can be recorded in a data chart or science notebook. Drawing and measuring the snails also scaffolded the observation objective. Rosa had participated in a snail study project in Spanish as part of her bilingual program training as a student teacher. She also drew from this experience for the design of her lesson cycle.

Rosa's Study, the Lesson Cycle, and Scaffolding

Rosa activated scaffolds related to each of the lesson activities while explicitly targeting language and cultural resources through project-based learning and authentic inquiry about snails. Below we revisit Rosa's instructional cycle, linking her instructional activities to the scaffolding framework. We conclude with a discussion of Rosa's co-constructed word wall as illustrative of a scaffold designed to facilitate rich description.

Rosa's Lesson Cycle and Scaffolding Goals

Rosa's lesson cycle offers a concrete way to illustrate how she addressed the challenge of moving students from a scaffolded contingent stage for learning to a fading process and some transfer of responsibility in writing descriptions. Here we note the ways Rosa scaffolded how to observe a snail, how to communicate what snails look like through description, and, in particular, how to use vocabulary relevant to the features characteristic of snails.

Direction maintenance. Keeping the learning on target, or direction maintenance, is characterized as support of students' metacognitive activities and defined as keeping the learner engaged with a targeted objective. Rosa kept learners on target by keeping the study of snails as the focus of the lesson cycle; each day had a different objective of inquiry linked to an artifact with new observations of the snails. All activities targeted learning more about snails and ways to support that inquiry. For example, on Day 1, Rosa targeted the shells as a distinctive adaptive feature and focused on color with snail photos in their environment and actual snails to study. Then she scaffolded the development of descriptive words through modeling and a co-construction of a word wall. In building the word wall, Rosa decided to provide some of the more technical terms that the children had not generated: apex, tentacles, respiratory pore, and shell lip. Some of these Rosa felt the students would need in order to measure the size of the shell (apex); others she knew the students would not be able to identify on their own.

Cognitive structuring. Teachers' explanations of why a technique or activity is useful have been called cognitive structuring (Tharp & Gallimore, 1988, p. 63). Rosa presented the study of snails as scientists' work, integrated with guided questions to investigate via data. For example, she requested students to measure the shell from apex to base to make decisions about snail size. Group feedback was provided through guided questioning to elicit how students approached measuring shells and estimating size. Rosa here focused on how scientists work with tools, including a magnifying glass provided for each pair.

Slicing down. Slicing down on the learning domain or objective for the learner, or reducing the degrees of freedom, is linked to support of students' cognitive activities and refers to when the teacher takes over of the parts of the task that the learner cannot yet do alone or without assistance from peers. For example, Rosa asked students to describe the snails' physical characteristics, with the scaffold of a co-constructed word chart, adding features or labels for those that were not known to the students and demonstrating to students how to combine color words in English to convey nuances of color (e.g., brownish black striped). Rosa modeled some examples and then asked students to generate others in groups outlining how *-ish* works with color in English. Students were able to generate many more color words with this scaffold (see Figure 2).

Rosa compared pre- and postdescriptions of the snails, looking at the number of different descriptors provided and their relevance. Figure 3 provides an overview of the changes in the number (N) of descriptors. Rosa summarized her findings in her inquiry report:

Baseline/outcome comparisons on the use of descriptive language in students writing about their snails showed improvement in the following ways:

(1) The N and percentage of descriptive words in the snail descriptions

(2) The adherence to the lead typical features of a snail description: size, color, movement, and multisensory features

(3) Aspects of form are still developing; all students used relevant descriptors but some still were exploring how to express size, for example, *medium* in Christian's description. Punctuation and spelling are still developing.

(4) Students increased the number and variety of descriptive words by substantial amounts, at a minimum doubling and in most cases showing increases of 500%.

Color	Size	Body Parts	Movement	Feel
Black	Small	Apex	Over	Nasty
Peach	Tiny	Foot	On Top of	Gross
Brown	Big	Shell	Slowly	Slimy
Dark-Brown	Large	Tentacles	In Circles	Gooey
Light-Brown	Skinny	Eye Spots	Straight	Ticklish
Yellowish-Brown	Fat	Mouth	All Over	Smooth
Black-Spotted	Little	Respiratory Pore	Up	Squishy
Green	Miniature	Shell Lip	Down	Cold
Tan			Sideways	Sticky
Dark-Brown Striped			Faster	Wet
Black Striped			Zig-Zag	Uncomfortable
Grayish-Brown				

Figure 2. Rosa's Word Wall as a Co-Constructed Scaffold

Student	Pre-Description	Post-Description
Andres	1	6
*Bianca	3	7
*Christian	1	7
*Oscar	1	6
Erik	2	3
*Alex	1	3
Alma	2	5
Jose	2	4
*Britney	3	6
Melanie	1	3
Rick	1	4
*Sam	1	4

*ELs

Figure 3. Rosa's Tally of Pre- and Postdescriptions—Charting Growth in Descriptors

Note: All names are pseudonyms

An example of an EL's progress from pre- and postdescriptions of the snails follows:

Pre: "The snail is very big."

Post: "My snail looks yellowish-brown *it *go's in slowly way with its foot, Something else I *noteiced about my snail is that is medium. Its foot is *tickleish and gooey." (Christian, an EL)

Recruitment. Motivating participation, or recruitment, is an affective goal that refers to how the teacher engages students with the task and helps them to adhere to the core requirements of the task. Rosa used think-pair-share with a peer, targeting "everything you know about snails" to prepare her students to contribute to a KWL discussion. She scaffolded the task by reducing the social demands by assigning roles and tasks to each member of the pair so that each child had an opportunity to ask a question and record a response. Here she accessed cultural resources by encouraging conversation in Spanish. She then recorded pairs' suggestions, using the word chart category system as a way to organize the information: color words under one column and so on.

Contingency and managing/frustration control. This affective goal of contingency and managing/frustration control refers to incentives the teacher might provide to keep students engaged with the targeted task. Rosa used a variety of ways to manage the degree of responsiveness of her lead scaffolds and manage frustration. For example, the use of descriptors relevant to snail descriptions would have been frustrating to ELs if she had not used a co-constructed word chart and deployed it strategically. First, the word chart served to explore ways to describe the snail shell in terms of color and shape, in the first observation. The inquiry about movement was supported in part by the familiar term *foot*. The call for a multisensory frame to observe the main snail body parts helped to scaffold how to report on what the shell and foot looked like and how these felt to the touch. Targeting the question: How big is my snail? Rosa added *apex* to the word chart as a scaffold to help students understand that the highest point, or apex, of the shell would be the end-point for measuring the shell from the ground up.

The means or tools of scaffolding address how teachers, parents, or helpful peers through their actions may support learners. These tools as outlined by Van de Pol et al. (2010) are self-explanatory and include (1) feeding back, (2) hints (also called prompting), (3) instructing, (4) explaining, (5) modeling, and (6) questioning. Rosa used all of these tools. Perhaps because this was the first inquiry for her students, modeling, explaining, and instructing were most prominent. She modeled behavior and explained her expectations for the class on how to work with the snails: creating a strict protocol for handling the snails, enlisting pairs of students to be responsible for a snail, giving feedback on the everyday care of snails and the need for washing hands after each session.

Scaffolding Language/Learning

Rosa was masterful in understanding that to develop a scientific understanding of description, her ELs needed to develop a greater understanding of how color and pattern descriptors function in English. Here Rosa relied on her understanding of language from her own experiences, her teacher research class texts (Gibbons, 2002, 2009), and feedback on her lesson cycle design. Gibbons (2009) provides multiple analyses of tasks and genres, identifying demands and illustrating ideas for scaffolding language across the curriculum. For example, factual genres relevant to science that Rosa could expand on with her students include (1) information reports—on land and sea snails, (2) procedures—how to raise snails, (3) procedural recounts—a recount of an experiment to see how snails can move across different surfaces, and (4) a temporal explanation—an account of a snail's cycle over a year.

Differentiating Demands of Contexts and Situations

In culturally and linguistically diverse classrooms, teachers must navigate how contexts and situations influence learning and understandings about the concepts targeted. Snail studies offer some fruitful opportunities for exploring the idea of snails as animals to study, a food source, or a pest. To explore these issues, Rosa could tap into analytical genres (Gibbons, 2009). For example, exposition/argument: how do people think about snails as a delicacy vs how do people who are growing a vegetable garden think about snails? This type of exploration could lead to another genre-type discussion. Students could then explore or debate how we should control snails in our gardens.

Supporting With Cultural Resources

Defining "cultural resources" and using these in culturally relevant pedagogy is a complex issue (Lee et al., 2013). Rosa identified parents as cultural resources in her snail study. She accessed parents' knowledge about snails but did not have the time to explore how prior experience with snails as pests might create a negative reaction toward them. The parents were instead recruited as informants who could expand their children's knowledge about snails. For example, Rosa's students were able to bring snails to the classroom by finding out from their parents when, where, and how they could find snails in their gardens.

Rosa was able to support her students with cultural resources more systematically by establishing a community of scientists conducting a study of snails in her classroom. The goal of the Snail Project was to capitalize on her students' curiosity about snails and channel their interest into a scientific exploration targeting scientific observation. In Rosa's study, the motivator for rich descriptions was to ensure that the description produced matched the child's snail and distinguished it from other snails. Children found that size and the nuances of the color of the shell were critical in fulfilling that function. The context of the situation in which descriptions are elicited clearly plays a role in how descriptions get constructed. The context of culture in Rosa's lesson cycle was the community of scientists. The children were paired as teams of scientists studying snails in their environment. Each member had a magnifying glass and a science notebook to record notes on all the lab work on snails. To be scientific, a description had to include details that were accurate and descriptive enough to help in identifying each team's snails. Some snail features were provided via guided questioning (the color mixes and patterns of the shells), some via instruction (the apex of the shell) to facilitate measurement and making an accurate drawing.

In Rosa's situation, many of her students had seen snails before, but they had viewed them as pests. In the situation of the inquiry of the class, Rosa had to establish rules for that community of practice. She and her students co-constructed a set of behaviors invoking a new set of rules when working with the snails as animals to be treated with respect. Rosa noted that initially some children had expressed some concern about working with the snails. However, once given explanation of lines of responsibility and reminders of their roles as scientists, all adhered to a respectful stance toward the snails they were studying.

Conclusion

In summary, Rosa seems to have successfully created productive scaffolds for those aspects of scientific observation and description that she targeted in her snail inquiry: observations of the snails' shells with illustrations and the co-constructed word chart as lead scaffolds. These scaffolds underwent fading from the baseline to the outcome data. In the limited time available, Rosa gave less stress to the instruction and fading of monitoring for the dispositions of scientific observation: attention to accuracy on reporting on size, for example. The disposition to observe and describe the shells accurately was cemented.

Building a Rationale for the Scaffolding Approach

Rosa identified multiple scaffolds to provide support for the snail lesson cycle, largely through the professional literature (Coleman & Goldston, 2011). She considered scaffolding techniques linked to illustration and visualization. She also worked to develop the dispositions characteristic of scientific observation. The word chart, gradually co-constructed over multiple days, was especially productive. Promoting joint construction of oral versions of descriptors helped students generate their own descriptions. Here, she adhered to Gibbons' (2002) lesson cycle very effectively in developing the field, or topic, of snails through observation. Rosa sought to facilitate positive transfer from Spanish to English, emphasizing the characteristics of Spanish color words that could be a bridge to English. Fading the word chart to partial removal would be a useful next step to follow up with another cycle, where a new set of features could be explored as a focus (e.g., how snails move over challenging surfaces). The descriptions students drafted were not always error free but communicated the key features of the snail in rich detail. Learning how to co-construct color combinations and integrate multi-kinesthetic qualities were generative benefits for future composing.

Rosa serves as an illustrative case of how teachers can scaffold the language of scientific observation. Rosa supported her students' maintaining the direction or goal of the activities through snail study as a project. She used cognitive structuring by establishing the classroom as a community of practice working in small groups to conduct multiple observations. This use of scientific teams supported the students affectively. She managed frustration by providing specific feedback and strategically redirecting students to the co-constructed word wall. Rosa scaffolded language demands by specifically targeting descriptive words that would help students in observation tasks. For example, she showed descriptors in her word chart clustered by semantic feature, in terms of size and color. Rosa's outreach to families in Spanish provided additional support by enlisting parents as expert farmers to contribute to the discussion of snail habits. This outreach also enriched students' vocabulary in Spanish.

Reflection Questions and Action Plans

Teachers may consider how to scaffold the language of inquiry by exploring other genres essential to the language of science. Observations might target how snails rely on their shells as camouflage in the environment. These explanations might then target observation linked to more complex concepts, such as adaptation. Alternative text types might explore how scientists must explain their procedures very explicitly. For example, to develop understanding of the purpose of replication, students could read exemplars of recipe formats or sports magazines and analyze the scaffolds used to make easy-to-follow procedural explanations for cooking or kicking a soccer ball.

Using the integrated scaffolding model (Table 2), teachers may want to reflect on the following sets of questions:

1. What alternatives to the types of scaffolding that Rosa provided would you suggest in a similar animal study? What types of scaffolding do you currently provide to your ELs? When and why do you select these practices? What examples of fading, or gradual removal of a scaffold, have you tried?

2. Considering the learning needs of your students and the tasks they will engage in, what types of scaffolding practices could you incorporate into your instruction for an inquiry project in science? Why do you think these practices are beneficial?

3. Observation as practiced by scientists requires careful note taking. Jane Goodall is well known as a scientist who relied on observation as a lead tool to investigate animal behavior. How might you use informative texts, featuring scientists' discoveries, to help students understand the value of observation and description in science?

4. Finding an informative text to support animal study is not always easy. Rosa wanted to find a picture book that would represent accurate scientific information while at the same time engaging the children in a storylike narrative. The National Science Teacher Association (www.nsta.org) publishes a list of "Outstanding Science Trade Books for Children" every year, typically in March. Review the selection criteria, and discuss the list for the latest year with colleagues. Then, consult with a colleague for ideas on criteria for selecting effective books that facilitate science learning for ELs. Develop your own criteria, and try out your list with a few sample books. Consider Pringle and Lamme's (2005) review of picture storybooks on science topics, and select a sampler of picture books to share with your class.

Acknowledgments

We are grateful to Rosa for permitting us to present her case study of teacher research to illustrate scaffolding as a integrated framework.

An Integrated Perspective on the Dimensions of School Communication

Sarah Capitelli, University of San Francisco

Laura Alvarez, Melrose Leadership Academy, Oakland, California

Guadalupe Valdés, Stanford University

When thinking about the academic achievement and success of ELs, the implementation of the new Common Core State Standards for English Language Arts and Literacy in History/Social Studies, Science, and Technical Subjects (CCSS for ELA/Literacy; National Governors Association Center for Best Practices & Council of Chief State School Officers, 2010) can be viewed in one of two ways: a set of standards that will make content and language learning even more inaccessible to ELs or an opportunity for educators to shift how we view language learning and teaching and its relationship to content. We see the implementation of the CCSS for ELA/Literacy as a real opportunity for change in the way that language learning and teaching has been conceptualized traditionally. Instead of separating the learning and teaching of language from content, the CCSS for ELA/Literacy offer an opportunity to view language learning and teaching from an integrated and relational perspective. Rather than a separate set of skills and functions to be taught and learned, language and language development can be embedded and a part of everything that students do in the classroom.

In this chapter, we discuss the language demands embedded in the CCSS for ELA/Literacy and the types of instructional experiences ELs need to have in order to meet the standards and have success in school. We provide an overview and explanation of the Integrated Perspective on the Dimensions of School Communication, which we believe is a helpful framework for understanding the language demands and opportunities for affordances in instruction. Finally, we exemplify this perspective by describing pieces of a second-grade earth science unit and a fifth-grade U.S. history example. These examples demonstrate the integrated nature of language and literacy and how the work children do with literacy depends upon and builds on the opportunities afforded to them to use language meaningfully in a diversity of ways.

What Kind of Language Do ELs Need to Develop to Meet the CCSS?

As schools begin to implement the CCSS for ELA/Literacy, a major question to consider is what kind of language do ELs need to develop to meet these new standards and succeed in school? It is clear that the standards are "language heavy" and require a sophisticated and diverse use of language, but what this language actually *is* is not as clear. Is it error-free language? Is it the language we hear native English speakers using? Is it academic language? It is difficult to answer these questions because it is not clear exactly what "academic language" is and what it looks like across grade levels and content areas. Academic language is often juxtaposed to everyday language or conversational language (e.g., basic interpersonal communication skills, or BICS, and cognitive academic language proficiency, or CALP). For example, we tend to associate academic language with content-specific vocabulary, grammatical complexity, and accuracy. However, academic English proficiency encompasses a diverse range of language abilities. Everyday language also plays a critical role in school learning, supporting students in accessing and communicating their prior knowledge, engaging with and making meaning of academic content, and serving as a pivotal link to the development of the formal academic language of various content areas (Gibbons, 2002, 2009).

Similarly, when talking about academic language, written language is often privileged over oral language. Producing error-free written language is seen by some as the ultimate academic exercise. Unfortunately, this dichotomy often serves to undermine writing by focusing more on the mechanics of writing and less on the ideas and content of writing. These ideas and content grow with a multitude of experiences, including critical oral language experiences, less formal written language experiences, and reading experiences with a variety of texts. This is of critical importance for ELs. When the writing instruction and opportunities privilege mechanics over content and ideas, it can limit the opportunities for ELs to develop their oral language and literacy abilities. ELs need to have substantial opportunities to engage in discourse around the ideas and content they are going to write about. This discourse helps to build their understanding of content and ideas, provides them opportunities to practice communicating their developing understanding of content and ideas, and creates opportunities to practice language functions (e.g., argumentation) before using them in their writing.

However, recognizing the crucial role that both written and oral language plays in students communicating their academic understanding is only the first step. It is also critical for teachers to recognize the relational uses of oral and written language in academic contexts (Horowitz, 2007). Within a single academic experience, for example, a class debate, students are asked to do a number of things with language that point to how interconnected the uses of oral and written language are. For example, during a class debate, students might refer to notes for their talking points that were produced during a lecture, video, whole-class or small-group discussion, or while reading a text. The lecture might have been a more formal presentation, but the group or small discussions might have included less formal talk. The notes might have gone through a series of iterations, beginning as a whole-group discussion and moving to a small-group conversation where critical ideas for the debate were discussed, synthesized, and articulated. Regardless of the series of experiences leading up to the debate, oral and written language experiences, both formal and informal, played critical roles in the academic experience, and these experiences built upon and off of one another. Teachers need to be particularly conscious about how they are building students' understanding of content and language and literacy competencies in their planning of instructional sequences.

CCSS and Specific Demands for ELs

For the purposes of this chapter, we focus on the Reading Informational Text, Writing, and Speaking and Listening Standards. These standards make it very clear that both content knowledge and the language needed to communicate this content knowledge need to be practiced and developed in order to meet the standards. For example, the CCSS for ELA/Literacy standard W.2.7 requires that students participate in shared research and writing projects in order to write a report, record their observations, and communicate their developing understanding. In our second-grade science unit, the content demands of this standard ask students to participate in a group experience in which they are documenting their observations during an investigation. The linguistic demand embedded in this experience requires that students have the language to communicate their observations both with their peers and the larger group. It is important to note that although the content and linguistic demands are the same for all students, regardless of their language level, the language that students use to meet these demands may be very different, given their language level. For example, an emergent language learner may use only one or two words to articulate his or her observations, labeling what he or she has seen with content vocabulary that has been developed, while a more advanced EL will use more complex language forms to communicate his or her observations. This is true for both oral and written language. For example, an emergent EL might need the scaffold of a cloze sentence to write, whereas a more advanced EL will be able to draw on familiar language structures to write.

Integrated Perspective on the Dimensions of School Communication

Bringing together the idea that oral language plays a critical role in academic achievement and language development for ELs and building on the overlapping relationship between written and oral language, we propose a working framework that integrates the four modalities of language: speaking, listening, reading, and writing. This working framework includes and recognizes the importance and need for both conversational and interactional competencies in school, as well as the importance of both productive and receptive proficiencies. It is our hope that this working framework can help educators move away from instructional practices that dichotomize language practices (e.g., BICS and CALP) and view language teaching and learning as separate from literacy and content.

An Integrated Perspective on the Dimensions of School Communication illustrates the three types of communication required to participate and achieve in academic contexts: interpersonal,

Table 1. An Integrated Perspective on the Dimensions of School Communication

	Interpersonal Communication	Interpretive Communication	Presentational Communication
Oral language	Used in face-to-face oral communication	Used in comprehending spoken communication as a member of class, audience, or other group	Used in communicating orally with a group (face-to-face or at a distance)
Written language	Used in informal written communication between individuals who come into personal contact	Used in comprehending written communication as a member of a general readership	Used in communicating in writing with an audience or general readership

interpretive, and presentational (Table 1).[1] Each type of communication takes into account the number and arrangement of the interlocutors involved (one-on-one or one-to-many, and face-to-face or at a distance) and the type of language skills (productive or receptive) required for the particular task. This integrated perspective highlights the relationship between the language modalities and content instead of isolating language use and development from content and ideas.

Additionally, an Integrated Perspective on the Dimensions of School Communication highlights the diversity of classroom experiences students need to have in order to communicate as well as the diversity of ways language is used in a classroom and the types of language competencies students need to develop in order to function successfully in a classroom (Table 2). These experiences also exemplify the inherent relationship between language development and content. This framework highlights the important role communicating understanding and meaning plays in the development of language. Ideas and meaning are privileged over isolated grammar instruction. The examples in Table 2 are meant to illustrate the kinds of experiences students have and need to have in academic contexts, but the list is by no means exhaustive.

Pedagogical Practices

In the remainder of the chapter, we focus on two examples from practice, one from a second-grade earth science unit and another from a fifth-grade U.S. history unit. Through grade-level examples, we show the integrated nature of language and literacy and how the work children do with literacy depends upon and builds on the opportunities afforded to them to use language meaningfully in a diversity of ways. We use the Integrated Perspective on the Dimensions of School Communication as a framework to exemplify the variety of experiences ELs need to have with language in order to practice and develop the sophisticated language practices required in achieving the new standards.

---

[1] For a more detailed discussion of the Integrated Perspective on the Dimensions of School Communication, please refer to Valdés, Capitelli, and Alvarez (2011).

Table 2. General Examples of an Integrated Perspective on the Dimensions of School Communication

	Interpersonal Communication	Interpretive Communication	Presentational Communication
Oral language	• Pair shares • Asking and answering questions of teacher and/or peers • Requesting assistance • Negotiating roles in a small group • Defending a position in a discussion • Explaining understanding	• Listening to a lecture • Listening to (watching) a video • Listening to peers give a presentation in class • Understanding instructions	• Presenting to the class • Participating in debates • Reporting on small-group discussions/work • Constructing visuals for class presentations
Written language	• Writing a note to a friend • Writing in a dialogue journal with a peer or teacher	• Reading texts (both print and online, fiction and nonfiction) • Collecting information from texts	• Writing a report, narratives, summaries, etc., for the teacher or peers • Editing and revising written work

Our Second-Grade Example: Vocabulary in Action

The following instructional sequence was designed for a second-grade class in an urban California district. The class consisted of 20 students, all of whom were ELs. The class was a late-exit Spanish-bilingual classroom, and science was a content area used for English language development (ELD). None of the students had been redesignated yet, and all had California English Language Development Test (CELDT) scores between 1 and 4. The class was working on an earth science unit to understand and develop several big ideas,[2] including

- the diversity of rocks based on different physical properties,

- the idea that smaller rocks are a result of the breakage and weathering of larger rocks,

- the diversity of the properties of soil, and

- the language to describe and communicate an understanding of these different physical properties.

These ideas were developed through opportunities for students to observe and investigate real rocks (W.2.7), participate in a variety of discussions about their observations and investigations (W.2.8,

---

[2] This unit is based on the California State Science Standards for Earth Science in second grade and was adapted from the Pebbles, Sand, and Silt Lawrence Hall of Science FOSS Unit. For more information about these standards and/or science unit, please refer to http://www.cde.ca.gov/be/st/ss/documents/sciencestnd.pdf and http://www.fossweb.com.

SL.2.1), and to read and be read to from informational texts (RI.2.1–3, RI.2.7–8). Students began the unit by observing a variety of rocks and understanding their various properties. Students used their everyday language to describe their observations, and a list of the various attributes was generated (SL.2.5). Students then had the opportunity to rub rocks, wash rocks, sort and classify rocks, and further describe the rocks and what occurred during their investigations. They developed the scientific vocabulary to describe and communicate their ideas and understandings about the properties of rocks (L.2.4). They then wrote a series of paragraphs comparing and contrasting the rocks they had observed and investigated, drawing on their hands-on experiences, discussions, and reading of informational texts (W.2.2, W.2.8).

Developing language through talk and text. The experiences described above are the initial part of the unit. The following lesson is situated in this first part of the larger unit. The children have already had the opportunity to explore a diversity of rocks in a variety of ways. They have used their everyday language to communicate their developing understanding and observations. The students are now given a sheet with the vocabulary and concepts shown in Figure 1, which are drawn from the unit on earth science as well as from the informational text the students read.

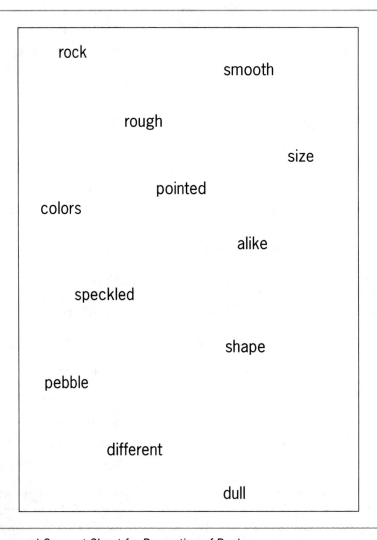

Figure 1. Vocabulary and Concept Sheet for Properties of Rocks

The teacher has created an identical class-size sheet that hangs at the front of the class. Along with the students, the teacher reads aloud the words and concepts on the sheet. The teacher then asks the students to make three connections between the words or concepts on their sheets, drawing a line to connect them (Figure 2).

She then has the students work with a partner and share the connections they have made between concepts and vocabulary. As students are sharing their connections, the teacher circulates among the pairs and listens for their ideas. She hears students saying things like, "Rough rocks aren't smooth" and "The rocks are different sizes" and "Our rocks were all different shapes." After the students have shared with one another, the teacher brings the students back together and asks them to share with the class some of the connections they made on their sheets. As students are sharing their ideas, the teacher makes the connections on the class chart. The students will revisit these vocabulary words and concepts to make additional connections after they read an informational text about rocks with the teacher.

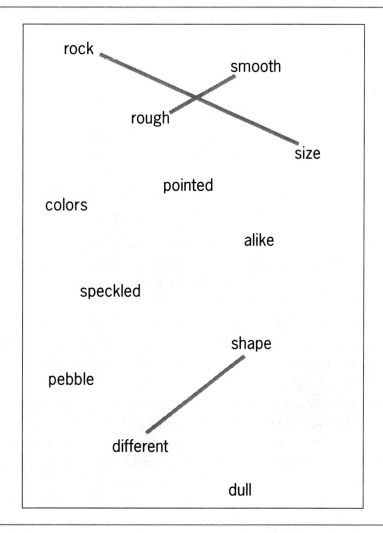

Figure 2. Prereading Example: Vocabulary and Concept Sheet for Properties of Rocks

This prereading (and eventually postreading) activity with vocabulary and important concepts is critical in helping ELs develop both their language and their conceptual understanding.[3] The first pass at the sheet enables students to use their prior experiences and background knowledge to make sense of potentially new vocabulary and concepts. It also provides productive and receptive oral language practice for students. Additionally, it is an activity that views vocabulary as something that can evolve and develop over time and through various experiences. Finally, it reframes academic language as *action oriented* (van Lier & Walqui, 2012) language that develops through experiences, meaningful use, and interaction with others versus something that can be taught and memorized.

Up to this point, the students have had a number of hands-on experiences investigating a variety of rocks. They now listen to the teacher read aloud a text, *Exploring Rocks* (FOSS, 2010), while they follow with a copy of the book they share with a partner. This book reinforces many of the concepts that students have previously explored (e.g., rocks can be grouped by different characteristics) and encourages the students to imagine a rock and describe it. During the readaloud the teacher stops frequently and reflects out loud on what she has just read, modeling the kind of thinking that good readers do while reading texts. This includes asking and answering who, what, why, when, and how questions (RI.2.1), and making connections between information in the text (RI.2.3) as well as connections between other texts they have read (RI.2.9) and the experiences they have had during the unit. In addition to sharing her own thinking, the teacher has the students talk with one another at various points during the readaloud, allowing students to ask questions or clarify their developing understanding (SL.2.1c), recount information they have heard/read during the readaloud (SL.2.2), and determine potential unknown vocabulary (RI.2.4). This experience with the text is more than a listening experience. The readaloud provides opportunities to engage in both content and language development. Students are reading, listening, and practicing their oral language skills while further developing their understanding of rocks. The experience both reinforces information and introduces new ideas and concepts while being scaffolded (RI.2.10) through teacher talk, teacher questions, and collaboration between peers.

After reading the text, the teacher has the students pull out their vocabulary and concept sheet and reread the words and concepts on the sheet, and then she asks them to make any additional connections between the words and concepts now that they have read the book. The students begin by working individually, making their connections before moving to work with a partner to share their new connections. The teacher circulates among the pairs, listening to their ideas. She hears students saying things like "Rocks are different colors like brown, pink, and white" and "Some rocks are dull and some are shiny" and "My favorite rock was speckled and smooth" and "We made pebbles when we rubbed the rocks together." The teacher also notices that the students are making connections between more than two words or concepts ("I put all the smooth rocks in a group and all the rough rocks in another group"). After students have shared with their partner, the teacher brings the group together and charts their new connections on the class chart (Figure 3). This whole-class experience gives students a chance to further articulate their ideas, as well as see new connections or reinforce connections they had already made.

---

[3] This exercise works with all types of activities, not just with reading activities. It can be done at the beginning of a larger unit or a single lesson, or before a hands-on experience or watching a video.

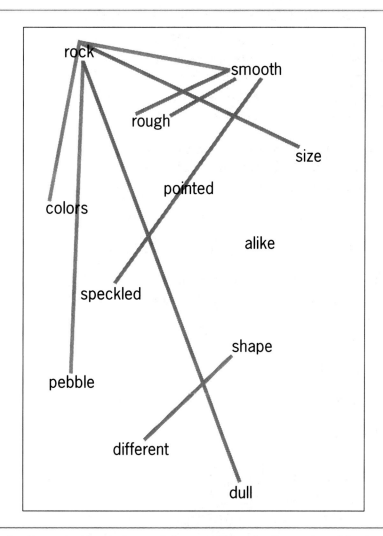

Figure 3. Postreading Example: Vocabulary and Concept Sheet for Properties of Rocks

Using talk and text to support writing. This series of experiences with new vocabulary and concepts provides a jumping off point for the writing the students then do to communicate their understanding of the various rocks they explored and the characteristics that make them different or alike. The talk that the students have done during their exploration as well as during the vocabulary exercise provides a pivotal foundation for their communicating about their ideas through writing. Students can draw upon a number of experiences where they have articulated their ideas and understanding to develop their writing: the readaloud/along, the rock exploration, the pre- and postvocabulary exercises.

Students choose their favorite rock to write a description about. The teacher tells them, as a class, they will remind themselves and brainstorm what they think should be included in a description of their rocks, such as color, texture, and size (W.2.8). Depending on the language level of the student, cloze sentences may or may not be provided (i.e., My rock is _____ and _____. My rock feels _____.).

After students have completed their written descriptions, the teacher pairs students together to scaffold a collaborative writing activity (W.2.7). The student pairs are asked to compare and contrast their rocks. Students read each other their written descriptions and then complete a Venn diagram describing the characteristics of their rocks that are alike and different. Finally, working in pairs, students write a description comparing and contrasting their two rocks (W.2.2, W.2.7–8). These descriptions are then shared with the class (SL.2.4).

This small sequence, contained in a much larger unit, highlights the number of ways in which language is used and integrated in the curriculum. The following steps enumerate the experiences described in the second-grade example:

1. Provide opportunities for students to observe and investigate real rocks.

2. Engage students in conversations about their observations.

3. Draw attention to particular vocabulary to discuss the properties of rocks and describe rocks. Make connections between the vocabulary based on students' observations and prior experiences.

4. Read and listen to informational texts about rocks and engage students in discussions around the details in the texts.

5. Revisit the vocabulary to make any additional connections.

6. Support students in writing informational texts (descriptions and comparisons) about rocks.

Additionally, Table 3 illustrates the number and variety of ways the students used language throughout the first part of the unit.

Our Fifth-Grade Example: Keep It or Junk It

The following instructional sequence was designed for a fifth-grade class in an urban California district. The class consisted of 30 students, three-quarters of whom are bilingual and entered school as ELs. In addition, one-quarter were African-American students, all of whom are native English speakers. The class was working on a social studies unit focused on Native Americans to understand and develop several big ideas,[4] including

- the similarities and differences between Native American tribes in different regions across the United States,

- the diversity in tribal regions and the impact of geography and climate on different tribes,

- how the arrival of Europeans changed the lives of Native Americans,

- how the arrival of Europeans had negative consequences for Native Americans, and

- conflicts between Native Americans and European explorers.

---

[4] This unit is based on the California State Science Standards for Social Studies in fifth grade.

Table 3. Second-Grade Earth Science Examples for an Integrated Perspective on the Dimensions of School Communication

	Interpersonal Communication	Interpretive Communication	Presentational Communication
Oral language	• Pair-share ideas about vocabulary and concepts • Explaining connections between vocabulary and concepts	• Listening to classmates share their ideas • Listening to teacher read the informational text	• Sharing connections with the whole class
Written language		• Reading the vocabulary and concept sheet • Reading or reading along with the informational text	

These ideas were developed through opportunities for students to observe and investigate pictures of Native American artifacts and a small number of actual artifacts (W.5.8), participate in a variety of discussions about their observations and investigations, including role-plays and debates (SL5.1), to read and be read to from informational texts (RI.5.1–3, RI.5.7, RI.5.10), and to write explanations about their developing understanding throughout the unit (W.5.7–8, W.5.9b, W.5.10). Students began the unit by sharing what they know and wanted to learn about Native Americans by completing a KWL (what we know, want to know, and have learned) chart. Students then had the opportunity to observe pictures of Native American artifacts (including housing, tools, utensils, clothing, and food) and a small number of real-life Native American artifacts. They used their everyday language to describe their observations (SL.5.4). They then had the opportunity to look closely at four different tribes in different geographical regions and learn about how the geography and climate of the region impacted the different tribes and how tribes managed these differences. This was done through reading both informational texts as well as investigating groups through Internet resources (RI.5.2–3, RI.5.7). Students developed the content-specific vocabulary to describe and communicate their ideas and understandings about the various native tribes (L.5.4). They wrote a series of paragraphs comparing and contrasting two of the tribes they had learned about, drawing on their hands-on experiences, discussions, and reading of informational texts (W.5.2, W.5.8).

In previous class sessions, students learned about the arrival of Europeans and the early explorations of the Americas. Through readings and a role-playing game, they learned about the cooperation and conflict that existed between the settlers. In this lesson, they begin to investigate the question, "Who benefited from the conflicts between Europeans and Native Americans?" by reading a selection from a challenging, grade-level history passage (Anderson, Jess, & Williams, 2000). The students' assessed reading levels range dramatically, and the teacher knows that many of her students need preparation and support to comprehend grade-level history text. However, she does not want to preteach key concepts and vocabulary from the text, because this would take away students' own opportunity to grapple with and work through complex text. Instead, the class spends approximately 15 minutes before reading considering the following scenario:

> You are a respected tribal leader. Until recently, you and your tribe have had a cooperative relationship with the colonists. However, you and your tribe are beginning to feel that your needs (e.g., food, shelter, land) are being threatened by the colonists. Your cooperative relationship with the colonists is becoming more contentious and a conflict seems inevitable. As one of the tribal leaders, you have to decide how to deal with the conflict.

> Which of the two options would enable you to protect the needs of you and your tribe?:

> 1. Engage in a war with the colonists in order to protect your needs and tribal land.

> 2. Compromise with the colonists, which means giving up areas of your tribal land.

In mixed language levels, groups of four students engage in lively discussions about which option they would choose and why, trying to convince each other so they can come to a group consensus (SL.5.1). The teacher selects students to share-out and facilitates debate across the groups (SL.5.4). Through these small-group and whole-class discussions, students have considered how conflicts escalate—a key concept for understanding how the arrival of Europeans had negative consequences for Native Americans.

Developing language through talk and text. Before reading the text, the teacher draws students' attention to the focus question (Who benefited from the conflicts between Europeans and Native Americans?), which is written on the top of the page. Because some students read far below grade level, the teacher first reads the text aloud as students read along silently. Students then work with their table partner to re-read the text and highlight key words and phrases that will help them answer the focus question (RI.5.2).

Once pairs have re-read and highlighted the text, they share out their list of key words and phrases. Having amassed a large list, the class then decides which words and phrases are essential to answer the focus question and which can be eliminated (L.5.4a).[5] Some words have been listed both as separate words and as parts of phrases that students chunked as carrying important meaning as a phrase. For example, students listed both "fighting" and "unaccustomed to fighting." For these cases, the class discusses which to keep on the list; in this case, they agree that "unaccustomed to fighting" is what is significant to who benefited from conflicts between Europeans and Native Americans. That is, Europeans benefited from the prolonged wars from the Native Americans not just because they were better at "fighting" but because the Native Americans were "unaccustomed to fighting" for such extended periods of time.

In other cases, students engage in contentious debates about whether a term is truly essential to answer the focus question, a process that helps the class clarify and hone in on the main ideas of the text (SL.5.4, RI.5.3). It is important to point out that this process and discussion are not focused on vocabulary, but rather on the concepts signified by the key words and phrases and how

---

[5] The reading task described here is known as Keep It or Junk It. A video example in a fifth-grade classroom can be seen at https://www.teachingchannel.org/videos/help-students-analyze-text.

they relate to one another in the text (L.5.4). Through discussing these terms, the students engage in discourse that collaboratively builds their comprehension of the text. Students' perspectives often change during the course of discussion, as they decide the group should eliminate a word they themselves had highlighted. The discussion is also text-based, and they return to the text multiple times to consider particular words and phrases and clarify their meaning in the context of the text as a whole. That is, the discussion of particular words like *tensions* and *exchanges* is not about their meaning in isolation or as defined in a dictionary, but about what it means in the historical events outlined in the text.

Finally, the class narrows the list to the following key words and phrases:

helped newcomers survive	~~forced~~
~~nurturing relationship~~	sachem
peace treaty	~~praying Indians~~
~~tension~~	shattered peaceful alliances
tension mounted	~~respectful relationship~~
~~forced~~	unaccustomed to fighting
land in high demand	~~disheartened~~
set up farms	illegal for colonists to sell guns to native people
colonists	~~fighting~~
Wampanoag	King Philip's War
exchanges	~~illegal~~
~~trading~~	600 colonists died
land trades	3,000 native people died
few blankets, coats, other supplies	native people enslaved
sections of land	people and resources greatly reduced
use the land	colonial government
own the land	northern colonies became more desirable
living things could not be owned	new industry developed
forced from lands	
~~endanger~~	

Students then work with their partners to place the words into the following categories:

Benefits for Europeans	Consequences for Europeans	Benefits for Native Americans	Consequences for Native Americans

Some words and phrases are placed in multiple categories. The class discusses the relationship between these categories and how they were interdependent and casually related, such that despite "peace treaties" between Europeans and Native Americans, "land trades" between them "shattered peaceful alliances" and led to serious conflicts. To conclude, students write their own explanations of who benefited from the conflicts between Europeans and Native Americans (W.5.2, W.5.8). Students are well-prepared to do so, having deeply processed the text and its content and having verbally articulated and heard their peers articulate the central ideas to the text. As they write, their categorized lists provide a concept bank and mapping of the key ideas of the text.

In the end, students have spent more than 2 hours in the whole process, from preparing to read, to highlighting and discussing key words and phrases, to categorizing terms, and, finally, writing. That is, 2 hours have been devoted to the study of two pages of text. However, this focused attention, reading, re-reading, and discussion is important to support students in developing their ability to comprehend such challenging texts.

This small sequence contained in a much larger unit highlights the number of ways in which language is used and integrated in the curriculum. The following steps enumerate the experiences described in the fifth-grade example:

1. Provide opportunities for students to observe and interact with Native American artifacts.

2. Engage students in conversations about their observations.

3. Have students read and listen to informational text about conflicts between Europeans and Native Americans.

4. Have students collaboratively identify key vocabulary and concepts in the grade-level text that contribute to answering key questions.

5. Provide opportunities to explain connections between vocabulary and key concepts.

6. Support students in writing informational texts (explanations) about European and Native American conflicts.

Additionally, Table 4 illustrates the number and variety of ways students used language throughout the fifth-grade example.

Reflection Questions and Action Plans

These two examples highlight the ways in which language, literacy, and content work together. Over the course of a student's career, the CCSS for ELA/Literacy spiral and build from the kinds of experiences students would have in the primary grades through middle and high school. These examples from practice highlight the variety of experiences students, and especially ELs, need in order to make sense of the language and content they are presented in school. The experiences in the second- and fifth-grade units move from more interpersonal to interpretive to presentational, as they learn grade-level content. The interpersonal experiences are foundational in preparing students to write and in students' processes of making sense of complex text.

Table 4. Seventh-Grade World History Example for an Integrated Perspective on the Dimensions of School Communication

	Interpersonal Communication	Interpretive Communication	Presentational Communication
Oral language	• Group discussion of scenario • Back-and-forth discussion of scenario • Partner discussion about which words to highlight and which words to keep or eliminate from the list • Debate about which words to keep or eliminate	• Comprehending other groups' ideas about the scenario • Comprehending others' ideas about key words and phrases	• Sharing out group discussion of the scenario to the whole class • Sharing out rationale for keeping or eliminating a word or phrase
Written language		• Reading history text and highlighting • Re-reading multiple times to decide on key words and phrases	• Writing explanations

The example also highlights the role of vocabulary and concepts but pushes educators to view these vocabulary and concepts as more than simply a list of words but rather a dynamic set of ideas that are firmly grounded in the disciplines students are learning. Making sense of such rich concepts requires more than simply studying vocabulary terms, but rather a variety of opportunities to engage with concepts through texts, hands-on experience, and discourse. Key to this learning is developing rich representations of how concepts are interconnected, and having many experiences to discuss these interconnections and hear others articulate these ideas as well. Through multiple experiences in print and discourse, students are able to make sense of such concepts and use them in meaningful ways in both their talk and their writing.

In reflecting on the chapter, consider the following:

• With a colleague, try using the Integrated Perspective on the Dimension of School Communication to think about your practice. Reflect on a unit of study that you currently teach (or are planning on teaching) in your classroom.

— What opportunities do your students have for interpersonal, interpretive, and presentational communication?

— What experiences do your students have before they are expected to use their presentational communication skills?

— Have you planned for adequate oral language experiences? Can you add any more to the unit?

Suggested Activities

- Create a Vocabulary in Action sheet for an informational text you are going to read with your students. Discuss the vocabulary/concepts that you chose with a colleague.

  — Why did you pick the vocabulary/concepts that you did?

  — What connections do you anticipate your students will make initially?

  — How does the text you are reading push their conceptual thinking and understanding?

- Identify an informational text you will use for Keep It or Junk It.

  — What elements of the text do you anticipate will be challenging for your students?

  — What written experience will students have after reading the text and engaging in Keep It or Junk It?

  — How will the text and the Keep It or Junk It experience push their conceptual thinking and understanding and support their language development?

Reconstructing, Deconstructing, and Constructing Complex Texts

Pamela Spycher, WestEd

Karin Linn-Nieves, San Joaquin County Office of Education

In this chapter, we share an instructional approach for supporting ELs in interacting meaningfully with complex texts in integrated English language arts and science. This approach supports ELs in the upper elementary grades (and beyond) to simultaneously develop academic English proficiency, literacy skills, and content knowledge. It provides a straightforward way for teachers to discuss how English works in particular ways in different texts and disciplines with their students, which promotes students' language abilities and language awareness. We highlight the specific Common Core State Standards for English Language Arts and Literacy in History/Social Studies, Science, and Technical Subjects (CCSS for ELA/Literacy; National Governors Association Center for Best Practices & Council of Chief State School Officers, 2010) content and language demands that this approach addresses and ground it in research and theory. We have used the approach in our professional learning work with elementary and secondary teachers, and we share some tips based on various successes and challenges encountered. Living in California, where we have new English language development standards (CA ELD Standards), we demonstrate how these standards are used in tandem with the CCSS for ELA/Literacy.

We provide some illustrative examples of our implementation of this approach in third- through fifth-grade classrooms, and we suggest some ways that might help teachers start using the approach with their own students.

CCSS for ELA/Literacy and Specific Language Demands for ELs

Clear instructional implications emerge from the CCSS for ELA/Literacy, including the critical need to emphasize meaning making when students interact with texts (both reading and writing them) from the earliest grades. These meaningful interactions include reading texts more analytically for different layers of meaning, being aware of particular language used in texts and how language choices affect meaning, discussing texts in intellectually rich ways, and recognizing the integral relationship between content and language. These meaningful interactions are cultivated in instructional environments that promote and nurture critical thinking, collaboration, creativity, and extended discourse about texts and topics that matter. Intertwined with all of these themes are motivation and engagement, as students are much more inclined to interact with texts and others when they see that tasks are focused on meaning making.

These instructional implications for meaningful interactions with texts and with others guided the design of the instructional approach we describe in this chapter, an approach that addresses multiple interrelated CCSS for ELA/Literacy. Like all students in the upper elementary grades, ELs learn to interpret complex informational texts, reading them closely and purposefully to build content knowledge (RI.3.10, RI.4.10, RI.5.10). They write informative/explanatory texts to examine a topic and convey ideas and information clearly (W.3.2, W.4.2, W.5.2). While writing informational texts, they apply their knowledge of language and its conventions (L.3.3, L.4.3, L.5.3), using general academic and domain-specific vocabulary (L.3.6, L.4.6, L.5.6) and expanding, combining, and reducing sentences for meaning, reader/listener interest, and style (L.5.3a). In addition to interpreting complex informational texts and writing their own informational texts, ELs learn how to engage in a range of productive collaborative discussions about content, where they share their ideas clearly, pose questions so they can learn different ideas and perspectives, and build on others' ideas, all the while applying their growing knowledge of respectful academic discourse (SL.3.1, SL.4.1, SL.5.1).

This cluster of CCSS for ELA/Literacy involves applying various comprehension strategies, listening to others' ideas, and writing and speaking effectively to express ideas. In addition to these content demands, it is important to be explicit about the language critical for successful engagement with complex texts and tasks. The language demands in the cluster of CCSS for ELA/Literacy highlighted above, particularly when science informational texts are involved, include the following:

- Knowing the meanings of general academic and domain-specific vocabulary while reading and selecting vocabulary carefully to produce precise meanings when writing or speaking.

- Disentangling meanings from long sentences and/or complex sentences (e.g., "As the red-eyed tree frog matures, it loses its ability to breathe under water with gills and develops lungs in order to breathe air").

- Expanding and enriching ideas in order to convey intentional and precise meanings (e.g., "They have long legs" → "They have long, powerful, jumping legs").

- Combining and condensing ideas in order to show relationships between ideas (e.g., "Bats are animals. Bats are mammals. Bats have live babies." → "Bats are mammals, animals that have live babies").

- Linking sentences throughout a text in cohesive and coherent ways using text connectives (e.g., *for example, however, finally*).

- Knowing what some words (e.g., *it, them, they, their*) refer to in long stretches of text (e.g., "**They** use **their** extremely long fingers and a wing membrane stretched between **them** to fly").

- Engaging in academic discourse about content, using specific language to gain and hold the floor appropriately (e.g., "I'd like to add something . . ."), acknowledge others' ideas while respectfully disagreeing (e.g., "That's an interesting idea. However . . ."), or prompt for clarification (e.g., "Could you explain that?").

Science informational texts have particular ways of using English, and when teachers are aware of these ways, they can make them transparent for their students (Fang, Lamme, & Pringle, 2010). For example, long noun phrases (e.g., "its ability to breathe under water with gills") enable writers to pack in a lot of information in a small amount of text, but these densely packed sentences can be difficult for students to navigate when reading and to produce when writing. Similarly, nominalization, which is the process of condensing information from one part of speech (usually verbs) into nouns or noun phrases (e.g., able → ability, survive → survival, frogs becoming extinct → frog extinction) begin to appear in science informational texts in the upper elementary grades. In science, nominalization is often used to gather information and repackage it in order to use it to further explain things or to sum things up (Schleppegrell, 2004). One challenge students may have is that the nominalized version of the word may be unfamiliar, and another is that these nominalizations create "lexically dense" texts (in other words, a high number of content words per total words), which can make it difficult for them to "unpack" the text's meanings. When teachers are aware of these types of language demands present in the texts students read, they are in a better position to empower their students by helping them develop knowledge about language so they may successfully understand complex texts. This knowledge enables students to be more successful in their analytical readings and interpretations of texts and more intentional about the language choices they make when they write or speak.

These interrelated content and language demands require teachers to think carefully and plan intentionally about how to teach their students about how English works to create meaning. Instruction that develops language and language awareness should build into and from content knowledge and content instruction in intellectually rich, engaging, and interactive ways where students have abundant opportunities to learn about language and also to apply their growing language skills, knowledge, and abilities in meaningful ways with rich texts and tasks. Such instruction supports students' comprehension while reading and listening to complex texts, while enabling them to make informed choices about using language when writing and speaking.

In California, where we work with teachers of ELs, the CA ELD Standards highlight and amplify the language skills, abilities, and knowledge about language of those CCSS for ELA/Literacy that are critical for ELs to simultaneously be successful in school and develop academic English. They provide guidance to teachers on designing instruction where students interact in meaningful ways through three "communicative modes"—collaborative, interpretive, and productive—and learn about how English works through three "language processes"—structuring cohesive texts, expanding and enriching ideas, and connecting and condensing ideas (California Department of Education, 2012). Because they were designed to be used in tandem with the CCSS for ELA/Literacy, both sets of standards informed the pedagogical approach we present.

Rationale

The instructional practices we present in this chapter respond to the dual and inextricably linked content and language demands of the CCSS for ELA/Literacy. The approach we share was inspired by the theory of systemic functional linguistics (SFL), which approaches "grammar" as an endless set of possible choices for making meaning with language and not as a set of rules (see Christie & Derewianka, 2008; Halliday, 1993; Derewianka & Jones, 2012; Schleppegrell, 2004). SFL has served as a rich and useful theoretical foundation for research in K–12 classrooms over the past several decades in many countries, including the United States (see, e.g., Brisk, Hodgson-Drysdale, & O'Connor, 2011; de Oliveira & Dodds, 2010; Gebhard, Willett, Jimenez, & Piedra, 2010; Gibbons, 2008; Pavlak, 2013; Rose & Acevedo, 2006). Research derived from SFL has demonstrated how, as students move from the primary into the upper elementary grades and beyond, the language used in the texts they encounter becomes increasingly complex. The texts become more densely packed with content information, and the language in them begins to shift from more familiar "everyday" registers to less familiar "academic" registers. The term *register* refers to the ways in which language resources (including vocabulary, grammatical structures, and discourse practices) are combined to meet the expectations of different situations. These expectations vary, depending on social purpose for using language (e.g., to explain, entertain, persuade), the content area and topic, the audience (e.g., talking with a friend, interacting within a professional community), and the mode in which the message is conveyed (e.g., spoken, written, multimodal).

Everyday registers in school are used to do things like chatting with a friend about a favorite book before writing about it, explaining to someone how to correctly play soccer, or any number of everyday school occurrences that do not require specialized language. Academic registers in school are used to do things like participate in a structured debate on climate change, write a science report based on a research project, or persuade the principal to allow students to use cell phones during class for specific learning activities. These academic activities require specialized language, and many students, including ELs, who may be unfamiliar with this way of using language, rely on school to help them develop it. Rather than thinking of everyday and academic registers as a dichotomy, it is more helpful to think about register choices as a continuum. As we engage in interaction with others along the "registers continuum," we select different language resources to meet register expectations. Derewianka and Jones (2012) provide a useful way of thinking about how our language changes as we shift from more "spoken-like" to more "written-like" modes of communication, presented in Figure 1.

Teachers can support their ELs in engaging in a variety of academic tasks across disciplinary areas by designing tasks that enable them to develop the linguistic resources that will allow them

Register	Everyday		Academic
	← - →		
Characteristic	More "spoken-like" language: spontaneous, dialogue, loosely packed with content information, flowing	Using both spoken-like and written-like language resources	More "written-like" language: planned, monologue, densely packed with content information, tightly structured
Examples of student actions	Discussing what's happening during a science experiment Jotting down notes during the experiment	Engaging in a collaborative discussion about the results of the experiment Writing a recount of the experiment in their science logs	Delivering a formal oral presentation about the experiment Writing a science explanation

Figure 1. The Register Continuum

Source: Adapted from Derewianka and Jones (2012).

to make informed register choices (Schleppegrell, 2013). By discussing the language resources available to students, teachers demystify academic language and remove the veil from the "hidden curriculum" of language (Christie, 1999). These language resources, which are given explicit attention in the Learning about How English Works section of the CA ELD Standards, include those useful for doing the following:

- Structuring cohesive texts (e.g., by using text connectives such as "for example" or "consequently" to create cohesive texts).

- Enriching and expanding ideas (e.g., by intentionally using precise general academic and domain-specific vocabulary such as *destroy, extinct, mammal,* and *species* or by expanding noun or adjective groups).

- Connecting and condensing ideas (e.g., by combining clauses in particular ways to show relationships between ideas).

Drawing students' attention to these language resources extends good teaching practices (including engaging students in rich discussions about content and in close readings of texts) by focusing on how language works to make meaning. The instructional approach we present next provides a way of highlighting and amplifying the language resources of complex informational texts that may not be readily transparent to ELs. It also gives students opportunities to apply their growing repertoires of linguistic resources in meaningful ways as they simultaneously develop content knowledge. The approach is particularly beneficial for ELs at the "expanding" or "bridging" level of English language proficiency (ELP, as defined in the CA ELD Standards) as it stretches students to use academic language and also think about how the language works to make meaning. However, the approach is equitable because it allows for students at any ELP level to engage in the tasks, with appropriate scaffolding provided by their teachers.

We'll share a mini-unit we developed in order to scaffold ELs' ability to read their science informational texts closely and write science explanation texts independently. We designed the mini-unit to be used in the context of a larger unit on animals, where students engage in collaborative, inquiry-based learning about an animal they choose, read many texts and research to learn more about it, discuss their learning with others, and work collaboratively to write reports and make presentations. In the series of lessons we share in this chapter—a mini-unit on bats—we focused on integrated science and ELA with a particular focus on English language development. On average, the lessons in these examples take 30–45 minutes to implement. While we've taught students using this approach and variations thereof in multiple classrooms in elementary, middle, and high school, we designed the illustrative examples we share here for third- through fifth-grade classrooms.

The examples we share in this chapter were drawn from work with a rural school in California's agriculturally rich central valley. The school's principal had requested coaching support from Karin (the second author of this chapter and a county office of education English learner specialist) in improving instruction for all students but especially for the school's Hispanic/Latino students (91% of the school's enrollment) and ELs (52% of enrollment). Nearly all of the school's students (92%) were eligible for free/reduced lunch. Just over 37% of the schools' students were proficient in ELA, according to the California Standards Test. At the same time, Pam (the primary author) had been sharing the work she'd been doing in schools across the state with other teacher educators and as a researcher in applied linguistics. We worked together to implement the approach in the school where Karin was providing coaching in order to demonstrate for teachers how the CCSS for ELA/Literacy and the CA ELD Standards work in tandem.

Instructional Approach

The main instructional approach featured in this chapter—text reconstruction and deconstruction—is contextualized in a "teaching-learning cycle," which is a useful organizing framework for planning units of study around science and history topics (Derewianka & Jones, 2012; Rose & Martin, 2012). In the teaching and learning cycle, attention to the organization and language features of texts is embedded in rich content instruction and intellectually engaging tasks using complex informational texts. In the teaching–learning cycle, teachers guide their students through four phases of learning the content knowledge of a topic and learning about the language used to convey the content knowledge. The four phases are (1) building content knowledge of the topic, (2) learning about the language of the text types, (3) jointly constructing texts, and (4) constructing texts independently.

Phase 1: Building Content Knowledge

As in all teaching, the first phase of the teaching–learning cycle focuses on meaning. More specifically, it centers on building students' content knowledge of a topic by providing ample opportunities for students to interact in meaningful ways with the content. One common science topic in third through fifth grade is the study of animals, not only their characteristics and behavior, but also their role in healthy ecosystems. Students build their content knowledge of this topic in a variety of ways (e.g., through inquiry-based practices, reading books, viewing multimedia, engaging in discussions, going on field trips, learning new vocabulary). Through these intellectually rich activities, ELs are learning English and learning through English.

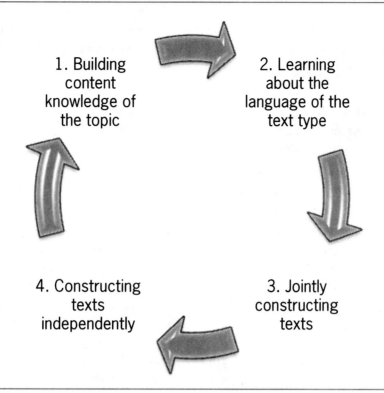

1. Building content knowledge of the topic

2. Learning about the language of the text type

4. Constructing texts independently

3. Jointly constructing texts

Figure 2. The Teaching and Learning Cycle

Source: Adapted from Derewianka and Jones (2012); Rose and Martin (2012).

In this first phase, one engaging way we've found useful to simultaneously build content knowledge, language, and literacy is "collaborative summarizing," based on the work of Klingner, Vaughn, and Schumm (1998). In collaborative summarizing, students work in pairs or small groups to read a short text passage (e.g., a text on animal habitats), discuss who or what the section is about and the most important thing(s) about the person or thing, and then collaboratively construct a summary statement of the section in 15 words or fewer. While this is mostly a reading comprehension instructional practice, this approach promotes not only close reading of text and interpretation of content, it also requires discussion between students and attention to particular language resources to create precise written summaries. This is an easy practice to implement, and once students get the hang of it, they have fun with the game-like challenge of manipulating language in order to convey precise content meaning with a limited number of words. Viewing short videos and discussing them in structured ways is another engaging way to build content knowledge.

Phase 2: Learning About the Language of the Text Types

In the second phase of the teaching and learning cycle, students delve deeper into language and learn about how it works to convey content knowledge. In this phase of the teaching–learning cycle, teachers draw their students' attention to the language of the text types being used in the unit of study (e.g., narratives, information reports, explanations, opinions/arguments). This phase is an opportunity to highlight and amplify the language features of the texts students are using to build content understandings. This could entail examining how a strategically chosen text is organized and how particular text connectives (e.g., *for example, in addition, however*) create cohesion or how particular text types have very long noun phrases that are useful for describing things. In our text reconstruction lesson below, we present an illustrative example from this phase of the teaching and learning cycle.

Text reconstruction. By this second phase in the teaching–learning cycle, students have been engaged in learning about bats and the critical role they play in the health of ecosystems. We analyzed the texts about bats students would read in order to identify the language demands of the text type and the language resources we wanted students to build up so they could use them in their speaking and writing when they wrote and presented on their own animals at the end of the unit. In the text reconstruction lessons, we provided students with an opportunity to collaboratively reconstruct a brief informational text about bats: an explanation about how bats help humans and why bats are in danger. For text reconstruction, we select an excerpt from a text students are already using, or we use text from another source. However, for this mini-unit, Pam wrote the text so that there could be a focus on particular content knowledge and language features, thereby ensuring that students were interacting with complex informational text that stretched both their content understandings and academic ELP.

We taught text reconstruction lessons over three consecutive days during which students reconstructed with a partner and in small groups the two stages (description in the first paragraph and explanation in the remaining paragraphs) of a short text on bats. In addition to the two main stages, the text was organized into three big ideas—what are bats, why are bats important, and why are bats in danger. The steps of the text reconstruction lessons are as follows:

Text reconstruction lesson
1. *Read once:* Teacher reads a short text (usually no more than 60 seconds) aloud while students just listen.

2. *Read twice:* Teacher reads the text aloud a second time while students listen and take notes (bullet points with one to a few words).

3. *Compare notes with a partner:* Students work with a partner to compare their notes and add novel information.

4. *Reconstruct text with small group:* Students work with the same partner and another set of partners (four students total) to reconstruct the text using their combined notes. (This can also be done in pairs.)

5. *Check and compare:* Teacher shows the original text to students and invites students to discuss differences or similarities between the original and their texts. Teacher points out some preselected language features or language challenges that emerged during Step 4 (e.g., vocabulary, verb tense, sentence structure).

In the first and second steps of the lesson, students need to listen attentively for key information and language. The content and language are familiar because students have been learning about the topic, but teachers may need to provide additional scaffolding for some or all students, depending on their needs (e.g., vocabulary with pictures, structured note-taking sheet). In addition, if students do not yet know how to take notes, it is a good idea to preteach how to do that. Otherwise, students may try to write full sentences. Figure 3 shows an example of a student's notes (with vocabulary scaffolding for the terms *wind turbines* and *extinct* provided directly on the student page).

In Step 3, students work with a partner to compare their notes. Each student shares what they wrote and adds novel ideas from their partner. This way, students have more information from the text than they would be able to record independently. In Step 4—our favorite step of this lesson—students form groups of four to reconstruct the text using their combined notes. The idea is not to replicate the text verbatim, but rather to reconstruct a text that conveys the content knowledge and incorporates as many of the language resources from the original text as possible. This gives students an opportunity to apply their knowledge of how English works and their skills using it. Students discuss their notes, determine which words and phrases are most important for conveying

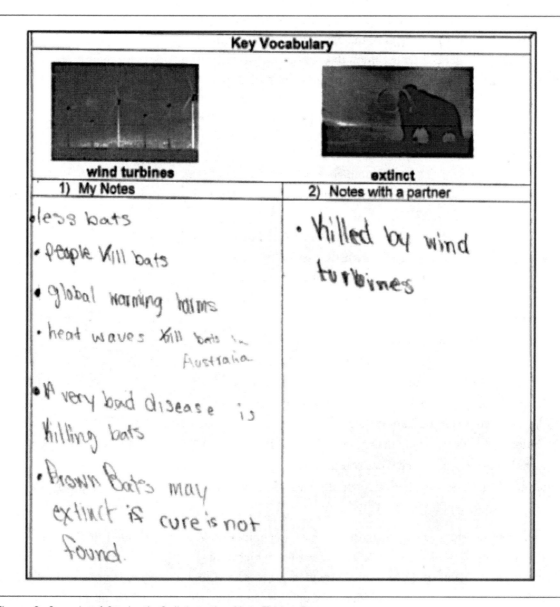

Figure 3. Sample of Student's Collaborative Note-Taking Page

the content, decide how to put the words and phrases together to form sentences, and determine the order of sentences so that the text makes sense. This step of the activity requires that students discuss the meaning of the text as they are constructing the language to convey that meaning because the information has to be expressed accurately.

During this phase, as students are working together to re-create a meaningful text from their notes, they are by necessity discussing the content while also using the new academic language of the text. Their collaborative conversations, therefore, simultaneously build content knowledge, comprehension of the text, knowledge of academic language, and writing proficiency. The task is also an ideal opportunity for us to observe how students are grappling with content knowledge and language, and we listen carefully to their conversations so that we can step in and provide scaffolding for content understandings and language development where appropriate. This is an excellent formative assessment opportunity, in particular to note the language strengths and challenges that emerge for immediate "micro-scaffolding" (Derewianka & Jones, 2012) or for subsequent instruction and further exploration. For example, when Karin was observing groups of fifth graders reconstruct the initial paragraph of the bats text, there were many opportunities to provide some micro-scaffolding while listening in on discussions about what to include from their notes. The following is an exchange she had with the one group of students:

Nhia: What did you say?

Sofía: I said, "There are vampire bats. There are fruit bats. There are tiny bee eating bats."

Carlos: You mean tiny bumblebee bats.

Nhia: He's right. They are bumblebee bats. [Sofía edits her notes.]

Karin: How can you combine your three short sentences naming different types of bats into one sentence?

Sofía: There are vampire bats and fruit bats and tiny bumblebee bats.

Karin: When you write and are listing several things, it is better to use a comma instead of *and* so many times. If I was writing about fruits, I would write, "There are apples – *comma* – oranges – *comma* – and berries." Try that with bats.

Nhia: Like this? [Writes and says the sentence aloud.] There are vampire bats, fruit bats, and tiny bumblebee bats.

Karin: Yes. What else is in your notes?

José: The bats are the only mammals that could fly.

Karin: Okay. In Spanish we often need to say the article before the noun "los" before "murciélagos," but in English we don't say "*the* bats." We just say "bats."

Carlos: Bats are the only mammals that could fly. [Everyone in the groups writes this.]

Karin: So re-read to me what you have so far.

Group in unison: There are vampire bats, fruit bats, and tiny bumblebee bats. Bats are the only mammals that could fly.

This example shows many instances of micro-scaffolding that Karin provided "just in time" for the students to be able to do something with it, which is an example of formative assessment in action. In fact, Nhia and Carlos also provided micro-scaffolding to Sofia when they helped her to transform "tiny bee eating bats" into "tiny bumblebee bats." This exchange is illustrative of the power of effective collaborative conversations (SL.3.1, SL.4.1, SL.5.1) and collaborative learning in general.

In Step 5 of the lesson, we guide students to compare their writing with the original text by showing the text on the document reader, and they enjoy seeing how closely their text reconstructions match the original text. Some students like to volunteer to show their reconstructed texts before we show them the original, and their willingness to take risks and discuss their writing in front of their classmates exemplifies the level of trust teachers establish in their classrooms. After students have had a brief chance to check the original text and discuss similarities and differences with their partner(s), we point out a few of the language features of the text type and of this particular text. We plan in advance which language features (e.g., general academic and domain-specific vocabulary, grammatical structures, text connectives, words for referring) we will highlight. However, during the lesson, we're watching and listening for any unanticipated challenges with particular language features; and if something emerges that many students need help with, we address it in this phase. For example, Karin noticed that several students were using the phrasing "Bats are the only mammals that *could* fly." She didn't correct José in the moment (see the example above) because she saw that it was a challenge that many students were having. In Step 5, when she showed the students the original text "they're the only mammals that *can* fly," she pointed out that the modal verb used in the original sentence was *can* and not *could*.

On another occasion, when Pam used the same text in a third-grade class, several of the partners wrote the following:

"Bats are mammals. Bats are warm blooded. Bats have long fingers and wing-membranes. Bats have live babies."

This provided an ideal opportunity in Step 5 to show students how using pronouns (e.g., using "they" to replace "bats" after the first time the word appears) refers the reader back to what was already said. Using "pronoun reference" is one way to create texts that flow and are easier to read (cohesion). These examples of formative assessment practices (observing what students are saying and writing) and micro-scaffolding (providing timely and selective feedback in the moment) are critical for moving students along the register continuum.

An example of the students' collaboratively reconstructed texts is provided in Figure 4.

Karin read the next two sections of the bats text on two subsequent days, following the same text reconstruction procedure. By the third day the entire bats text had been reconstructed.

Next, we had students read the entire original text closely in its entirety in an interactive and engaging way in order to prepare them for the upcoming *text deconstruction* activities. We used a Split Dictation activity (Gibbons, 2009), where two students chorally read two different versions of the same text and where each version of the text had different words missing. In this barrier "game," each partner was responsible for sharing the missing words with his or her partner, ensuring that his or her partner wrote the correct words and spelled them accurately. Partners re-read the text to make sure each had a completed version of the text, because they would be using it for subsequent deconstruction activities. Here is an example of the first two sentences from the Split Dictation activity:

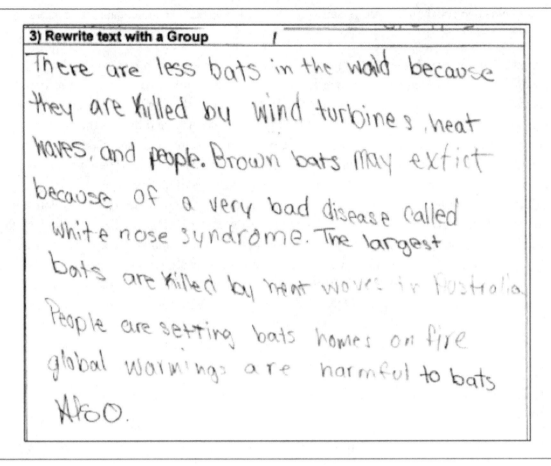

3) Rewrite text with a Group

There are less bats in the wold because they are killed by wind turbines, heat waves, and people. Brown bats may extirt because of a very bad disease called white nose syndrome. The largest bats are killed by heat waves in Australia. People are setting bats homes on fire global warmings are harmful to bats Also.

Figure 4. Sample of Students' Collaboratively Reconstructed Text

Partner A's text:

Bats are _____, animals that have live babies, are warm-blooded, and usually have _____ on their bodies. There are over 1,200 bat species, or different kinds of bats, in the world.

Partner B's text:

Bats are mammals, animals that have live babies, are _____, and usually have hair or fur on their bodies. There are over _____, or different kinds of bats, in the world.

Text deconstruction. Students were now ready to delve deeper into the language features of the text and deconstruct it further so that they would have a better understanding of the language in the text. For deconstruction activities, we often (but not always) start by focusing students' attention on text organization and how different text types are structured the way they are in order to achieve particular social purposes (e.g., to entertain, explain, describe, persuade). For example, the bats text is an explanation, and explanations are organized logically around big ideas, following a predictable text structure with the general stages of "description" and "explanation." Figure 5 shows the stages (description, explanation, conclusion) and phases (what are bats, why are they important, why are they in danger) of the bats text, along with content details in the phases to point out to students.

Stages and Phases	Text
Description What are they? • Identification • Classification • Physical characteristics	**What Are Bats?** Bats are mammals, animals that have live babies, are warm-blooded, and usually have hair or fur on their bodies. There are over 1,200 bat species, or different kinds of bats, in the world. For example, there are fruit bats, tiny bumblebee bats, and even vampire bats. Bats make up about one-fifth of all mammal species, and they're the only mammals that can fly. They use their extremely long fingers and a wing membrane stretched between them to fly. The bat's wing resembles, or looks like, the human hand.
Explanation Why important? • Eat pests • Spread pollen • Saliva used to make medicine	**Why Are Bats Important?** Bats are extremely important to the health of our natural world, and they help people in many ways. Most bats, about 70% of them, eat insects. These bats hunt and eat many insects that are harmful to people, like mosquitoes or insects that destroy the food growing in fields and on trees. A single little brown bat can eat up to 1,000 insects in a single hour. About 30% of bats eat nectar or fruit, and when they do, they help spread pollen and seeds so that more plants can grow. We wouldn't have all the food we do if it weren't for bats spreading pollen and plant seeds. In fact, many plants would die off completely if it weren't for bats. About 1% of bats eat fish, mice, frogs or other small animals. Only three species feed on blood. But it's not as scary as it sounds. They lap it like kittens rather than sucking it up as horror movies suggest. Even these bats are useful: Something in their saliva, or spit, is used to treat humans who have had strokes, a very serious illness.
Why in danger? • People hurt them • Global warming • Disease	**Are Bats in Danger?** The number of bats in the world today is less than it used to be. The greatest threat to bats is people. Some people are afraid of bats and kill them by setting fire to their homes, killing thousands of bats. Other bats are killed by wind turbines that are placed along routes where bats travel. Global warming may also be harming bats. Over the past 15 years, 30,000 flying foxes—the largest bats in the world—in Australia have died from heat waves. Finally, an extremely bad bat disease, or sickness, called White-Nose Syndrome, is killing many bats in the United States. The little brown bat could become extinct from this disease if scientists can't find a cure.
Conclusion	We should help bats survive because they're important to humans and to the health of our world.

Figure 5. Bat Explanation Text Showing Text Organization and Structure

We show students this organizational structure by deconstructing the text, that is, showing the text on the document reader, re-reading the text with students, leading them in a discussion about the big ideas in the text, and marking up the text so that students can see where the big ideas appear. This helps to reveal the "stages" of the text. For example, in the bats text, which is an explanation text type, the sections are already clearly demarcated, and we intentionally wrote this text this way as a scaffold to show students what the big ideas are. It's not always this easy to find the big ideas, and students will need to work with texts that have less obvious organization and structure, but knowing what to look for helps. When we discuss text structure and organization, we find it particularly useful to highlight the text connectives (e.g., *in addition, however, for example, finally*) that help create cohesion in the text. Knowing about text organization and text connectives helps ELs navigate through texts and gives them ideas for making their own texts more cohesive.

In addition to text structure and organization, we delve deeper into various language features of the text that allow the writer to expand and enrich ideas. We teach general academic vocabulary (e.g., *destroy, resemble*) and domain-specific vocabulary (e.g., *species, mammal*) purposefully and intentionally so that students feel confident using the terms in their own speaking and writing. For example, when we teach the word "destroy," we contextualize the word by reminding students where they saw the word (in the bats text), provide a student-friendly explanation of the word (e.g., "when you destroy something, you ruin it or break it completely") along with multiple examples of how to use the word meaningfully in other contexts (so they don't think it is only used when discussing bats). We have students use the word in a brief exchange with open sentence frames when needed (e.g., "Insects might *destroy* the plants if/when _____") and structured think-pair-share to ensure equitable interaction (Beck, McKeown, & Kucan, 2013; Spycher, 2009).

Because understanding how English works involves much more than text organization and vocabulary, we also teach students about grammatical structures. This involves "unpacking" some of the long noun or adjective groups in sentences to disentangle the meanings in them, identifying the words that refer readers backward (or forward) in the text, and discussing any nominalizations we encounter. It also includes discussions about what's happening with verbs and verb phrases in different text types. In science descriptions and explanations, for example, verbs tend to be in the "timeless present" (e.g., Bats *are* . . . , Bats *eat* . . . , Bats *have* . . . , Bats *can* . . .) because they are conveying information about phenomena or groups and not what individuals did (e.g., The bat ate . . .). The types of verbs used in different text types varies, and we point out to students that because the bats text is a science explanation, the types of verbs they see in it are primarily being/having verbs (e.g., *are, have*), used for classifying or describing characteristics of bats, and action verbs (e.g., *use, help, hunt, eat*) used for describing or explaining behavior. In contrast, stories tend to have a lot of saying verbs (e.g., *said, whispered*) for dialogue between characters, and action verbs for showing what characters did, all in the past tense.

Phase 3: Jointly Constructing Texts

In the third phase of the teaching–learning cycle, jointly constructing texts (see Figure 2), we guide students to co-construct a text with us. We act as the "scribe," writing what the students say, but our role is also to strategically and purposefully guide students' journeys along the register continuum, supporting them to move from more spoken-like to more written-like language. For example, if we are jointly constructing a text with students, and a student offers "bats go out at night," we might prompt them to use a more precise term by asking, "what's the scientific word we use to mean animals that go out at night?" (nocturnal). For the bats unit, we typically jointly construct an explanation text because we've been working with students to reconstruct and deconstruct this text type. However, because students have been learning about why bats are important and why they're in danger, we also like the idea of jointly constructing a short opinion piece about why we should help bats survive. This builds on the concluding sentence in the original text while giving students some practice with constructing opinions/arguments.

Phase 4: Constructing Texts Independently

In the last phase of the teaching–learning cycle, students are ready to write their own texts independently with confidence, because they have been prepared to do so. Throughout the teaching–learning cycle, they practice, through additional scaffolded activities, how to write many different types of text. For example, in Phase 1 (building content knowledge of the topic), students might write brief descriptions of bat behavior in their science journals as they watch videos or short summaries of the texts they read. In Phase 2 (learning about the language of the text types), they reconstruct and deconstruct texts about bats. In the Phase 3 (jointly constructing texts), the students jointly construct a novel text with the teacher. All of this prepares them to write their own

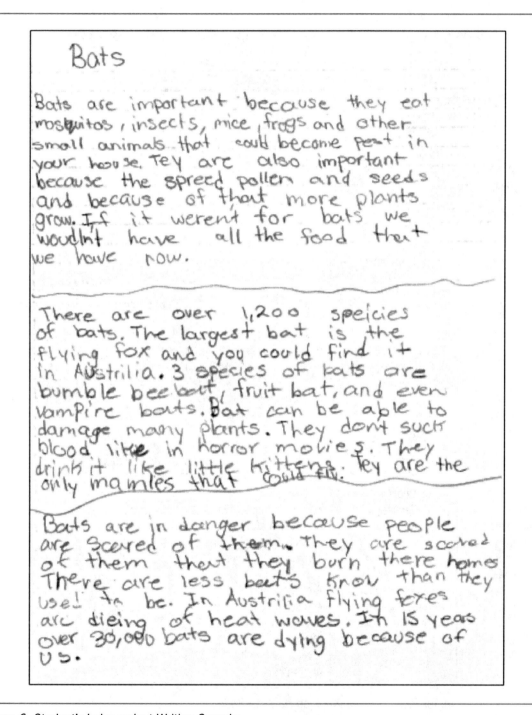

Figure 6. Student's Independent Writing Sample

texts independently. Figure 6 shows an example of a student's independent writing at the end of the bats unit.

It is helpful for students to receive specific feedback on their writing so they know what to refine and improve. We created a framework for providing feedback to students on their writing (Figure 7), which we adapted from the work of Gibbons (2009) and others for teachers to consider when they develop rubrics for assessing the writing of their ELs.

The rubrics teachers develop can draw from the CCSS for ELA/Literacy and their state's ELD standards in order to support their ELs at different ELP levels to advance along the register continuum.

Final Thoughts

When students become more conscious of how language is used to construct meaning in different types of texts, they have a wider range of language resources to draw upon when interpreting and creating texts, enabling them to make appropriate language choices. After teaching the text reconstruction lessons to a group of fifth graders in a new teacher's classroom, Karin reflected on how the teacher began to see her students as engaged and enthusiastic readers and writers.

Content Knowledge & Register	Text Organization & Structure	Grammatical Structures	Vocabulary	Spelling and Punctuation
Is the overall meaning clear? Are the big ideas there, and are they accurate? Is the text type (e.g., opinion, narrative, explanation) appropriate for conveying the content knowledge? Does the register of the writing match the audience?	Is the purpose (e.g., entertaining, persuading, explaining) getting across? Is the overall text organization appropriate for the text type? Are text connectives used effectively to create cohesion? Are pronouns and other language resources used for referring the reader backward or forward?	Are the verb types and tenses appropriate for the text type? Are noun phrases expanded appropriately in order to enrich the meaning of ideas? Are sentences expanded with adverbials (e.g., adverbs, prepositional phrases) in order to provide details (e.g., time, manner, place, cause)? Are clauses combined and condensed appropriately to join ideas, show relationships between ideas, and create precision?	Are general academic and domain-specific words used, and are they used accurately? Are a variety of words used (e.g., a range of words for "small": little, tiny, miniscule, microscopic)?	Are words spelled correctly? Is punctuation used accurately?

Figure 7. Framework for Providing Feedback on Student Writing

Source: Adapted from Derewianka (2011), Gibbons (2009), Spycher (2007, 2013).

One boy in the class, Miguel, who is labeled as "struggling," absolutely shone in his ability to lead and facilitate his group's interactions about the content they had just learned and the reconstruction process. Observing Miguel engaged in reading and discussing a complex informational text and then reconstructing it with others made his teacher see him with a new lens.

When we see our students interacting in meaningful ways with complex texts and discussing the way language works to make meaning, our perceptions of students expand, and our notions of commonly accepted terms, such as "struggling readers," are challenged. The promise of the CCSS for ELA/Literacy and other next-generation standards is to elevate our expectations of what our students can do and to give us the inspiration to continuously grow in our professional understandings so that we can support them in meeting those high expectations.

Reflection Questions and Action Plans

1. Which practices in this chapter affirmed what you already do? What was new for you?

2. How might the instructional approaches presented in this chapter promote your ELs' meaningful interactions with complex informational texts?

3. How might the instructional approaches in this chapter support your ELs' understandings of how language works to make meaning?

4. Which practices can you see yourself integrating into your existing practice?

Suggested Activities and Planning Tips

Try the five-step text reconstruction approach presented in this chapter with your students:

1. Use the tips below to guide your planning.

2. Teach the lesson and enjoy the process.

3. Take notes on what was successful for you and your students and what was challenging.

4. Using your notes, decide what you will refine the next time you teach a text reconstruction lesson and determine what your next steps will be.

Tips for intentional planning to make the language of texts transparent to students:

1. *Know your students:* Consider what your students already know about language and what they can do with language.

2. *Analyze the text:* Preread the text students will use and identify the text type, organizational structure, and language features.

3. *Set language goals:* Think about the language you want your students to be able to comprehend and produce.

4. *Be selective:* Determine which language features you will highlight to make transparent to students.

5. *Plan for engagement:* Determine how you will actively engage students so that they are interested in learning about both language and content.

6. *Plan to reflect and assess:* Decide how you will know if your lesson was successful. How will you evaluate student writing and provide feedback? How will you adjust your instruction?

6

Scaffolded Language Analysis

Danielle Garegnani, Sherman Elementary School, San Diego, California

The Common Core State Standards for English Language Arts and Literacy in History/Social Studies, Science, and Technical Subjects (CCSS for ELA/Literacy; National Governors Association Center for Best Practices [NGA] & Council of Chief State School Officers [CCSSO], 2010a) emphasize that students develop literacy and language proficiency in ELA and across content areas. In order for students to develop literacy and language proficiency, they need opportunities to participate in academic discussions about grade-level texts and topics, multiple opportunities to read and engage with complex texts, and practice writing the text types of different content areas. These opportunities are all grounded in reading, writing, speaking, and listening and are carried out through the understanding and use of language.

NGA & CCSSO (2010b) recognize that ELs should be held to the same high expectations as native English speakers but may need additional time and support to reach the standards. This will require teachers to adjust instruction and provide specific support, modeling, and opportunities to interact and use the language necessary to access and meet the standards (NGA & CCSSO, 2010b). The content demands of the CCSS for ELA/Literacy for Grades 3–5 require students to read and comprehend grade-level informational texts in which they determine main ideas and supporting details, describe overall text structure, explain how reasons and evidence are used to support points in a text, and discuss and write about grade-level informational texts and topics in which they demonstrate a command of standard English grammar (RI.3.2; RI.4.2, 4.5; RI.5.2, 5.5, 5.8, 5.10; SL.3.1; SL.4.1; SL.5.1; W.3.2; W.4.2; W.5.2; L.3.1; L.4.1; L.5.1). These standards place challenging, linguistic demands on our ELs such as understanding the grammatical features and patterns and specific word choices that help shape the meaning of a text; identifying and understanding the language features that signal relationships between events, ideas, or concepts; and understanding language functions, or how language is purposefully used, in different contexts when writing, speaking, reading, or listening. ELs need to understand these features of academic language in order to comprehend and interpret information in both listening and reading, and convey their understanding of that information through speaking and writing. The approach described in this chapter addresses these language demands to ensure students meet the CCSS for ELA/Literacy.

The CCSS for ELA/Literacy outline the standards to be taught but does not, however, give direction on how to teach the standards. How best to teach the standards in a way that addresses ELs' needs will have to be determined by teachers. Addressing these needs will require "increased teacher scaffolding and knowledge of the nature of text and language and how to scaffold conversations around text" (Pearson & Hiebert, 2013, p. 14). Therefore, content knowledge alone is insufficient; teachers will need to know the language features and understand the language demands of academic texts along with their pedagogical implications in order to support ELs' linguistic needs within ELA and other content areas.

As teachers, we need to create a supportive environment that will foster understanding and use of academic discourse across the domains of speaking and listening, reading, writing, and language. This chapter describes an instructional approach called *scaffolded language analysis* that we can take to support ELs in reaching the CCSS for ELA/Literacy. This approach is designed to raise student awareness of the linguistic features of different genres and engage students in discussion about the language of different text types. By analyzing language in texts and scaffolding student discussion about that language, we equip our students with the language resources they need to meet the CCSS for ELA/Literacy.

Rationale

The CCSS for ELA/Literacy call for literacy and language development across the content areas; language is the medium through which students accomplish academic tasks across grade levels and content areas by speaking, listening, reading, and writing (NGA & CCSSO, 2010a). Scholars in education agree that many ELs lack the understanding of academic language functions, which refers to the purpose for which we use language to accomplish tasks, and the language or grammatical features that help carry out these tasks (Dutro & Moran, 2003; Scarcella, 2003; Schleppegrell, 2004). For example, the purpose of a procedural text is to instruct. The language features that help accomplish this purpose include imperative verbs (commands such as *put, place, add*), sequential connectives (e.g., *first, then, after*), and modal auxiliary verbs (e.g., *should, must, may*). Each of these language features have different functions; imperative verbs function to explicitly direct the listener/reader what to do, sequential connectives function to indicate the order in which something takes place, and modal auxiliary verbs function to indicate the degree or importance of obligation in the task.

Different academic texts and content areas have specific grammatical or language features that help construct meaning of the text or content area (Schleppegrell, 2004; Gibbons, 2009). To understand and produce the language of the different text types called for in the CCSS for ELA/Literacy and in other content areas, students need to know what those language features are. ELs on their own are not likely to acquire and use academic language by simply listening to or reading about academic topics or texts. ELs need support in accessing and engaging with texts (Bunch, Kibler, & Pimentel, 2013). Having opportunities to develop awareness of and use academic language in school supports ELs in developing academic registers (Schleppegrell, 2012, 2013). By developing students' metalanguage, the language we use to describe and talk about language, we make language more visible, draw attention to how grammatical features work in context, and have ways to describe and explain how language works for particular tasks (Gibbons, 2009; Knapp & Watkins, 2005; Schleppegrell, 2004).

As teachers, how can we raise our ELs' metalinguistic awareness, develop their metalanguage, and scaffold their use of academic language to effectively accomplish academic tasks across grade levels and content areas in speaking, listening, reading, and writing? Talking about the language of different text types with our students is the first step in apprenticing them to use the language of different content areas. By highlighting and explicitly teaching the language features of different text types in context, we expand our students' linguistic repertoire by giving them the language they need to participate in academic conversations and accomplish tasks. We can foster dialogue and utilize guiding questions so students can analyze the language features and their functions of different text types. This helps students move from spoken-like, informal language use to more written-like, academic language use (Gibbons, 2002).

Education scholars recognize the importance of language analysis activities in classroom practice and have highlighted the ways in which teachers can make the academic language of complex texts more accessible to ELs. For example, Girard and Spycher (2007) explain how lifting sentences from texts, highlighting an example sentence from a core text, can help teachers show how sentences are constructed, helping students analyze information conveyed through different parts of the sentence. Similarly, de Oliveira and Dodds (2010) describe how "language dissection" of science texts helps teachers address the dense language of science and provides ELs a way to read and interpret difficult language to access the meaning of texts. Likewise, Fillmore and Wong-Fillmore (2012) illustrate how leading students through the deconstruction and discussion of sentences from complex texts helps students become aware of the language patterns and functions in texts and supports them in accessing the information embedded in complex language. By analyzing different language features and their functions in context, we can engage ELs in discussion about the meaning of a text or topic, and scaffold their comprehension and use of the language of the text type. This gives students opportunity to participate in extended academic conversations about a text, helps us gauge the extent of their understanding, and can signal when and where misunderstanding occurs, allowing us to respond or intervene when comprehension breaks down.

It is critical that we not only know our content but also know our texts well, in order to raise our ELs' awareness and understanding of different text types and guide them through discussion about their language features. We need to understand the language demands of the content we teach and carefully analyze the specific language patterns that students encounter in reading and are required to use in writing (Californians Together, 2010).

Teachers who understand the lexical, grammatical, and discourse features of academic English and how to make these features explicit to their students in purposeful ways that build both linguistic and content knowledge are in a better position to help their students fulfill their linguistic and academic potential. (California Department of Education, 2012, p. 7)

It is important that we are familiar with our texts and content area so that we can scaffold discussion and engage students in activities that highlight the way in which different text types have specific language features that add to the meaning and the purpose of the text.

The next section outlines an instructional approach, scaffolded language analysis, in which teachers can raise students' metalinguistic awareness through dialogue about the language features of different text types. The section describes activities and provides classroom examples and resources to help teachers plan for scaffolded discussion about the language of different text types ELs are required to read and write as reflected in the CCSS for ELA/Literacy.

Pedagogical Practice

Scaffolded language analysis is developing metalanguage through class discussion about texts. Each activity is intended to raise awareness of the linguistic features of different text types and engage students in dialogue about how those language features help us understand a text. This supports their comprehension of the text and highlights the different language choices students have when talking about or writing in a specific genre. There are several steps to scaffolding language analysis for students, which include:

Step 1: Planning for language analysis—identifying the challenging language in texts

Step 2: Reading and discussing the text with students

Step 3: Introducing the language features and analyzing language in context

Step 4: Engaging students in activities to scaffold use of the language features

Step 1

Before engaging students in language analysis of a text, we first need to look closely at the texts we use with students. An important aspect of text-based discussion is to understand the text type, the author's purpose for writing the text (i.e., to explain, to describe, to inform, to entertain, to persuade) and the language features that are common or specific to the text type. Some questions to ask as you plan for instruction are

- What type of a text is this?

- What is the author's purpose? What does the author want us to know?

- How is the text organized?

- What are the salient language features or patterns evident in the text?

- What is the domain-specific and general academic vocabulary in the text?

- Is there any content, vocabulary, or text feature that may pose a problem for my ELs?

Figure 1 identifies some of the language features of descriptive text types and provides examples from texts. This chart can help support instructional planning; once the overall purpose, structure, and language features are determined, planning for discussion around the text can be carried out.

Text Example	Purpose	Grammatical Feature	"Kid Language"
Most of the volcanoes in the world <u>are</u> composite or stratovolcanoes. Dome volcanoes <u>have</u> thick, slow-moving lava that forms a steep-sided slope.	**Description** To describe, classify, and define characteristics	**Linking verbs** is/are, has/have	Who or what is the sentence about? What is the sentence telling us about ____? Is the sentence telling us what ____ has, is, or does? What language/word tells us that the author is *describing*?
Hawaiian lava usually <u>gushes out</u> in red-hot fountains a few hundred feet high that <u>feed into</u> lava rivers or lakes.	**Description** To describe behaviors or capabilities	**Action verbs** can/could + verb	Is the sentence/paragraph describing what ____ is, has, or does? What is the action/word that tells us that? What does ____ do?
Old lava flows are quickly weathered <u>by the waves into rocks and black sand</u>.	**Description** To add information about frequency, manner, location, purpose	**Prepositional phrases** **Adverbial phrases** in/on/by/into/for phrases	What words/chunk of information give us more information about ___? Does the _____ chunk of information tell us about: When _____? Where _____? In what way _____? How _____?

Figure 1. Chart for Analyzing Some of the Language Features of Informational Texts

Source: Adapted from Knapp and Watkins (2005), Schleppegrell (2004), Gibbons (2002). Text examples from *Volcanoes* (Simon, 1988). This chart is an excerpt that provides a few examples. For more detailed explanation and examples of other grammatical features/text types, see Knapp and Watkins (2005).

The grammatical features included in Figure 1 provide some of the typical language found in descriptive informational texts. The column labeled "kid language" includes prompts and questions, which call attention to specific grammatical features and their purpose in the text, that can be used to guide students through language analysis of a text.

Step 2

This step focuses on students' gaining an initial understanding of the text. Prior to introducing and analyzing the language features of informational text types, it is important that students have read and discussed the text at least once, in order to become familiar with the text and understand the gist. Reading independently first gives students the opportunity to think about the text before moving on to more analytical reading. Next, re-read the text with students and guide a more in-depth group discussion about the text in order for them to gain a better understanding of the topic. Pose guiding questions before, during, and after reading to support students' understanding of the text. Questions to consider while reading may include

- What is the text mostly about?

- What are the main ideas of the text? What are some of the details of the main ideas?

- Why did the author write this text? What does he/she want us to learn?

- How is the text organized?

This phase of the instructional approach supports the Key Ideas and Details and Craft and Structure strands of the CCSS for ELA/Literacy Reading Standards for Informational Text (e.g., RI.3.1–2, 3.5; RI.4.1–2, 4.5; RI.5.1–2). Once students have a general understanding of the text, they are ready to begin discussing the language features.

Step 3

The next step in the instructional approach focuses on highlighting the language features of the genre and analyzing them in context through guided discussion. To raise awareness and scaffold understanding of the language features of a text type, introduce the different language features, one by one or a few at a time (this depends on the text itself), and highlight their use in the text. The sample classroom charts in Figures 2 and 3 illustrate how the language features of descriptive and causal explanation texts might be introduced and explained to students.

Descriptive texts describe, define, classify, and categorize information

Descriptive texts use language features such as

    is/are to define and classify (Lions are mammals.)

    has/have to describe attributes (Lions have manes.)

    action verbs to describe behavior or actions (Lions sleep during the day.)

    can + verb to describe abilities (Lions can roar loudly.)

    adjectives to add description to attributes (Lions have dark manes.)

    adverbs to describe the manner in which things happen (Lions quietly stalk prey.)

    prepositional phrases to add details about direction, location, or time (Lions sleep during the day in their dens.)

Does the sentence tell us what _____ is, has, does, or is like?

Figure 2. Descriptive Text Chart

Causal explanation texts explain how or why, or how and why, something happens

Signal words that link ideas together in causal explanations include

CAUSE—the reason	EFFECT—the result
Because . . .	As a result . . .
Due to . . .	_____ results in . . .
Since . . .	Then . . .
When . . .	Therefore . . .
If . . .	Consequently . . .
On account of . . .	
The reason for . . .	

Figure 3. Causal Explanation Text Chart

After introducing the language features, revisit the text with students to analyze the language features. Read through the text again slowly, sentence by sentence or paragraph by paragraph, prompting students to take notice of how language is used in context. Ask students how the grammatical features add to the meaning of the text and how individual words, phrases, clauses, or "chunks of information" help them understand the text better. Examples of teacher prompts and questions to guide language analysis are included in Figure 1 in the column labeled "kid language." Grammar can be intimidating, and elementary teachers may be uncomfortable using grammatical terminology with younger students. The purpose of the analysis activity is not to have students name parts of speech or label grammatical parts, but to raise their awareness of the language features of different text types and draw attention to how they are used in context. By doing this, we raise our students' metalinguistic awareness and add to their academic language toolbox. A major goal of the CCSS for ELA/Literacy is that students engage in close reading of texts and, by analyzing the language features, read parts of text multiple times to examine how meaning is carried out through the language.

The following classroom examples demonstrate how I guide fourth- and fifth-grade students through discussions about the language features of descriptive text during their English language development lessons. The students have read and discussed several mentor texts (descriptive and causal explanation texts) on frog endangerment and have been developing their understanding of the topic. Each lesson lasts approximately 20 minutes, and "instructional highlights" from typical lessons (provided below) illustrate the language analysis activities of this approach.

Instructional highlight #1. This English language development lesson begins by drawing on prior lessons about the different language features of descriptive texts. Some of the language features that make up descriptive texts include relational verbs *is/are/has/have*, which classify, define, categorize, and describe attributes or characteristics. Action verbs are also a feature of descriptions and are used to describe behaviors or capabilities. Furthermore, relative clauses (*that, which, when, who,* and *where* clauses that follow a noun) also add description or identify nouns in academic texts. Using an excerpt from a text read in prior lessons, we read the text again out loud on the document camera, discussing the language features of the text. The chart for descriptive texts (see Figure 2) is posted so that all students can refer to it as I ask them about the language of description used in the text. The text reads

> Different kinds of frogs have different kinds of feet. Frogs that live in or near water have webbed toes on their hind feet. The webbing helps them swim quickly through the water.

I begin by focusing students' attention on the meaning of the first two sentences and the language features that signal description. I then draw students' attention to the purpose of the relative clause "that live in or near water," which is to identify the frogs that have webbed toes and distinguish them from other frogs that don't live in or near water. Then, I confirm students' statements and indicate the relationship between the noun (frogs) and the relative clause (that live in or near water). Figure 4 provides an example of the text with my modeled annotations.

Ms. Garegnani:	[Reads aloud] "Different kinds of frogs have different kinds of feet." What is this sentence describing? What they do, what they have, or what they are?
Fernando:	What they have. Different kinds of feet. [Teacher circles "have" in the sentence.]
Ms. Garegnani:	[Reads aloud] "Frogs that live in or near water have webbed toes on their hind feet." What is this sentence doing?
Sarai:	Describing, telling that frogs have webbed toes. [Teacher circles "have" in the sentence.]
Ms. Garegnani:	All frogs have webbed toes?
Sarai:	No, just some. Only frogs that go in the water.

Are All Frog Feet the Same?

Different kinds of frogs have different kinds of feet. Frogs that live in or near water have webbed toes on their hind feet. The webbing helps them swim quickly through the water.

Flying frogs, which glide from tree to tree, have

Figure 4. Text Analysis of Shared Reading

Ms. Garegnani:	What is the *that* chunk of information doing? [Re-reads aloud the relative clause] ". . . that live in or near water."
Fernando:	Telling us only some frogs because not all frogs live in the water.
Ms. Garegnani:	Yes, the *that* chunk adds information to or identifies the noun before it. [Underlines the relative clause "that live in or near water" and draws an arrow to "frogs."]

When we analyze the third sentence (The webbing helps them swim quickly through water), I call attention to the description of the webbed toes, and prompt students to clarify their responses by asking what the sentence specifically describes. I then gauge their understanding of the reference *webbing* to *webbed toes* and indicate the relationship between the two nouns.

Ms. Garegnani:	[Reads the next sentence aloud] "The webbing helps them swim quickly through the water." What is this sentence describing?
Cristian:	Telling what the frogs do.
Ms. Garegnani:	The frogs? What specifically about the frogs does the sentence describe?
Edith:	The frogs' feet. It tells what the webbing does.
Ms. Garegnani:	What does the webbing do?
Edith:	Helps them swim fast. They're action verbs. [Teacher circles "helps them swim."]
Ms. Garegnani:	Where did *the webbing* come from? What is that?
Edith:	It's talking about their webbed toes. [Teacher underlines "the webbing" and draws an arrow to "webbed toes."]

This part of the discussion highlights how I support students' understanding of referencing, the way information is introduced and expanded on in a text, by explicitly asking about the webbed toes. Referencing builds cohesion in texts, and ELs may not always see the relationship between the two ideas, therefore causing comprehension to break down. We end the lesson with a discussion about how these three sentences introduce a main idea about frogs' different feet, and then give details about water frogs having webbed feet that help them swim, to support the main idea. In addition to addressing Reading Standards 1 and 2 for Informational Text, which focus on key ideas and details, scaffolded language analysis supports state language development standards such as analyzing language choices, understanding noun and verb phrases, understanding reference, and modifying sentences (see the California Department of Education, 2012, ELD.PI.4–5.6–7, ELD.PII.4–5.2–5).

After we engage in analysis and discussion of the language features of the text, students work independently or in pairs to analyze short excerpts of text read in class. Students highlight, circle, and underline language features specific to descriptive texts. This activity is fun and engaging for students because they have built up language awareness and become "language detectives," exploring and analyzing the meaning the language is expressing in their texts.

Step 4

The next step of the instructional approach aims to engage students in use of the language features of the text type. Sentence frames or sentence stems can scaffold ELs' oral and written production of language. Sentence frames and stems support ELs' language output by focusing on the grammatical form and sentence structure to fulfill a language task. Figure 5 illustrates sample sentence frames/stems that can be used to support the language of description. For example, relative clauses (*that, which, who, where* clauses) add description to or define the nouns that precede them, whereas prepositional phrases add information about time, space, or location. These language features are characteristic of descriptive texts, and by providing different sentence frames with grammatical variations, we draw attention to the linguistic choices available to students to successfully engage in academic conversations or writing.

To carry out this activity with students, introduce the sentence frames with the language features (Figure 5) and model their use with examples from the text being analyzed. Students practice creating sentences using the sentence frames and stems, either as a whole group or with partners. Afterward, elicit sentences from students and write them on the board or a chart. After a student shares the sentence, ask another student to add more information to that sentence, or give a different sentence using different language features that convey similar information. Write the second sentence down. Then, guide a class discussion about the how the meaning changes with the modification of the language feature. Engaging students in this activity helps them meet Language Standard 1, as well as language development standards that focus on interaction and learning about how English works (see California Department of Education, 2012, PI.4–5.1–4, 7, 10; PII.4–5.4, 5, 7). The following instructional highlight illustrates how students use the support of sentence frames and stems to modify sentences by adding description using different grammatical features.

Instructional highlight #2. In this part of the lesson, students expand and modify sentences to describe frogs. Figure 5 illustrates different sentence frames and stems to support the language work of this activity. I begin the lesson by explaining how different language features, such as prepositional phrases and relative clauses, can help us condense information and add description to a sentence. The following excerpt shows how I prompt students to add description to sentences that describe frogs.

_____ is/are _____.

_____ has/have _____.

___ (noun) ___ ___ (action verb) ___.

___ (noun) ___ can ___ (action verb) ___.

when _____	over _____	so _____
which _____	under _____	to _____
that _____	on _____	for _____ -ing
who _____	in _____	in order to _____
where _____		

Figure 5. Sentence Frames/Stems for Description—Sentence Construction

---

Ms. Garegnani:	We can add more details to descriptions by using prepositions and *that*, *which*, *who*, and *where* chunks. Who can describe frogs using one of the sentence frames?
Elizabeth:	Frogs have long toes that can wrap around twigs.
Ms. Garegnani:	Can we add another chunk of information to this sentence?
Alex:	Use which. Which helps them climb up trees.
Ms. Garegnani:	[Writes the sentence.] So our sentence says: "Frogs have long toes that can wrap around twigs, which help them to climb up the trees." What other language choices do we have [points to the sentence stems]?
Aline:	Tree frogs have sticky toes which help them to cling to trees and bark.
Ms. Garegnani:	Can we use a *that* or a *to* chunk?
Fernando:	Trees frogs have long, sticky toes that wrap around twigs to help them climb trees.

The discussion ends by reviewing how the language features (*that/which* clauses and prepositional phrases) add description and highlighting how the students are able to construct and modify sentences to add information with the support of the sentence frames. Examples of the expanded sentences created in this lesson are included on the classroom chart in Figure 6.

After we create sentences together as a group, students work in pairs to write sentences using the sentence frames to add or modify information about the topic they are describing. Figures 7 and 8 illustrate sentences students created to describe frogs or other animals using the sentence frames.

> We can expand sentences to add more description by using prepositions and that/which chunks of information.

• Tree frogs climb.	• Tree frogs **have** long toes <u>that wrap around twigs, which help them to climb trees</u>.
• Tree frogs have suction pads.	
• The suction pads stick to leaves and bark.	• Tree frogs **have** long, sticky toes <u>that wrap around twigs to help them climb trees</u>.
• Tree frogs are light.	
• Tree frogs hold on to branches.	• Tree frogs **have** suction pads <u>on their feet, which help them stick to leaves and bark so they can climb trees</u>.
• Tree frogs have long toes.	
• The toes are sticky.	
• The toes can wrap around twigs.	

Figure 6. Classroom Chart Showing Expanding Frog Sentences

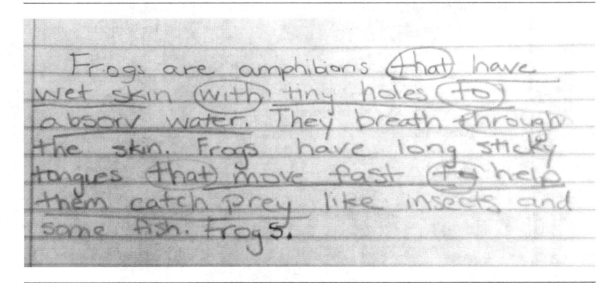

Figure 7. Student Sentences—Descriptive Text

Figure 8. More Student Sentences—Descriptive Text

The instructional activities described in this chapter support the development of metalanguage of ELs through scaffolded language analysis. Scaffolded language analysis addresses several of the CCSS for ELA/Literacy and California state English language development standards. This instructional approach requires students to read parts of informational text closely and multiple times, and determine main ideas and supporting details. It highlights text structure and the relationships between sentences and paragraphs, how specific word choice and grammatical features shape the meaning of a text, and how knowledge of language functions supports comprehension of text. This approach offers flexibility and supports language instruction across the curriculum. Language analysis can be incorporated as "mini" language lessons embedded within literacy, science, or social studies instruction or directly to support ELA instruction during dedicated English Language Development time. When we highlight, explicitly teach, and discuss the various language choices that create different types of texts, we develop our ELs' metalanguage and provide them with language resources to help them attain the CCSS for ELA/Literacy.

Reflection Questions and Action Plans

1. Reflect on the instructional routine for literacy in your classroom. How might some of the activities described in this chapter be integrated into your literacy instruction? Which activities could be easily incorporated? Discuss with a colleague.

2. How might scaffolded language analysis support ELs' understanding of science or social studies content? Discuss one way in which the activities presented could support ELs' understanding of science or social studies texts.

Action Plans

Action Plan 1. Analyze several informational texts with which your students will be working during language arts, science, or social studies.

1. Choose a short passage or paragraph from a text that may be challenging for students.

2. Using the charts in Figures 1 and 2, choose one feature to discuss with students.

Action Plan 2. Plan a lesson in which you guide students through language analysis of the text for one language feature.

1. Read and discuss the text with students (refer to Step 2 in this chapter).

2. Prepare a chart to introduce and teach the feature (refer to Figure 2).

3. Using Figure 1, develop questions to raise students' awareness of the language feature.

4. Guide students thorough an analysis of the language feature using the text.

Suggested Reading for Further Inquiry

These professional books and articles include in-depth explanations about the literacy challenges for ELs and include teaching strategies and activities that explain and extend the instructional scaffolds described in this chapter.

Freeman, D., & Freeman, Y. (2009). *Academic language for English language learners and struggling readers: How to help students succeed across content areas.* Portsmouth, NH: Heinemann.

Gibbons, P. (2009). *English learners, academic literacy, and thinking: Learning in the challenge zone.* Portsmouth, NH: Heinemann.

Girard, V., & Spycher, P. (2007). Deconstructing language for ELs. *Aiming high resource.* Santa Rosa, CA: Sonoma County Office of Education.

Heartbeats: Reading Informational Text in Depth in Grades 3–5

Linda New Levine, ESL/EFL Consultant

The CCSS and ELLs

One significant shift in Grade 3–5 reading programs under the Common Core State Standards for English Language Arts and Literacy in History/Social Studies, Science, and Technical Subjects (CCSS for ELA/Literacy; National Governors Association Center for Best Practices [NGA] & Council of Chief State School Officers [CCSSO], 2010) is the requirement for increased reading of informational text. In Grade 4, expectations are that students will balance their reading of literature (50%) with reading of informational texts (50%) in the social studies, sciences, and arts (National Assessment Governing Board, 2008). Although fewer than 10% of elementary English language arts texts are nonfiction (Duke, 2004), there are benefits to increased reading of these texts. Informational texts are content-rich and can be appealing to many children interested in the world of nature, geography, and history. And they acquaint children with unique vocabulary and grammar forms needed for future academic learning.

For the ELL population, however, the value of reading informational text may be overshadowed by reading challenges. Unknown vocabulary and sentence structure, limited background information, and differing cultural contexts may limit comprehension for many young ELLs. In addition, the CCSS for ELA/Literacy applies additional rigor to the reading of informational text.

The CCSS for ELA/Literacy for informational text are grouped into three areas of learning for each grade level. The first three standards relate to Key Ideas and Details in the text. In Grades 3–5, these standards are not dissimilar to current teaching practices in many elementary classrooms. The standards require students to ask or respond to questions concerning explicit details of the text.

Many teachers refer to these as recall, or "right there," questions. In addition, students are asked to isolate the main idea of the text and details supporting that main idea. This, too, is a component of many elementary reading classrooms. Additionally, students are asked to explain what happened in the text and why. The major difference in the Key Ideas and Details standards is that students are now asked to refer back to the text and explicitly refer to textual details. They may re-read the text several times in order to paraphrase, summarize, cite, or explain the meaning of the passage. Because ELLs may not be proficient readers of grade-level informational text, the requirement of locating and comprehending textual detail presents an additional burden. As students proceed through the grades, the language requirements of these standards become more complex. For example, Grade 3 students simply answer questions, recount, and explain. But students in Grades 4 and 5 are required to summarize (paraphrase) the text, a skill that is more difficult for ELLs, in that it involves reading a text for comprehension while determining and retelling the key elements of the content. ELLs will benefit from teacher scaffolding of these components to offset the dual-memory load of language and content. The standards in Figure 1 relate to Key Ideas and Details for informational text that are discussed in this chapter.

The second group of CCSS for ELA/Literacy relates to the Craft and Structure of the text. These standards take teachers and students into areas that have been little explored in Grades 3–5 reading classrooms of the past. Craft and Structure standards for informational text require students to determine meanings of academic words and phrases, compare and contrast structure and organization of two or more texts, and analyze multiple accounts of events or topics. These standards require a deep understanding of the language of the text and a very thorough understanding of the meaning of the text. Many students will be challenged by these standards, but ELLs will be the most challenged because they have a narrower understanding of the craft and structure of the English language.

Grade 3
RI.3.1 Ask and answer questions to demonstrate understanding of a text, referring explicitly to the text as the basis for the answers.
RI.3.2 Determine the main idea of a text, recount the key details and explain how they support the main idea.

Grade 4
RI.4.1 Refer to the details and examples in a text when explaining what the text says explicitly and when drawing inferences from the text.
RI.4.2 Determine the main idea of the text and explain how it is supported by key details; summarize the text.

Grade 5
RI.5.1 Quote accurately from a text when explaining what the text says explicitly and when drawing inferences from the text.
RI.5.2 Determine two or main ideas of a text and explain how they are supported by key details; summarize the text.

*Figure 1. CCSS for ELA/Literacy for Informational Text—Key Ideas and Details
(NGA & CCSSO, 2010, p. 14)*

Figure 2 lists selected Craft and Structure standards at Grades 4 and 5. The RI.4.5 and RI.5.5 standards both address the notion of text structure. The difference between them is a matter of degree. Grade 4 students describe the structure of a part of or all of one text. By Grade 5, students compare/contrast two texts. Similarly, RI.4.6 and RI.5.6 address point of view. Grade 4 students compare various accounts for focus and information provided. By Grade 5, students analyze multiple accounts comparing similar points of view.

The last three standards for informational text require the Integration of Knowledge and Ideas. Students in Grades 3–5 interpret information from many sources (media, web pages, graphs, diagrams, etc.) in relation to the information in the text. They compare several texts on similar topics, and they explain how the author uses reason and evidence to support a particular point of view. Once again, these are challenging tasks. ELLs are cognitively capable of all of them, but they will require differentiated instruction to master these rigorous standards.

Language Demands of Informational Text

In addition to the reading demands of the CCSS for ELA/Literacy, ELLs are challenged by the language demands of the standards. ELLs achieve most efficiently when language instruction integrates all four of the language skills: listening, speaking, reading, and writing (Grabe & Stoller, 2002; Tsang, 1996). Each skill scaffolds learning for the other. For example, oral language interactions requiring listening and speaking help students to intake new vocabulary and language structures— the input needed to increase textual comprehension and promote academic writing.

When considering aural/oral language demands, it is helpful to think in terms of the forms of the language as well as the functions. Language forms include the verb tenses, active and passive voice, compound and complex sentence structure, and other components of grammar. Language functions, on the other hand, relate to the purposeful use of language: asking and answering questions, explaining, recounting, and summarizing. The CCSS for ELA/Literacy are replete with language functions: describing, reporting, comparing, analyzing, quoting, retelling, and paraphrasing.

Grade 4
RI.4.5 Describe the overall structure (e.g., chronology, comparison, cause/effect, problem/solution) of events, ideas, concepts, or information in a text or part of a text.
RI.4.6 Compare and contrast a firsthand and secondhand account of the same event or topic; describe the differences in focus and the information provided.

Grade 5
RI.5.5 Compare and contrast the overall structure (e.g., chronology, comparison, cause/effect, problem/solution) of events, ideas, concepts, or information in two or more texts.
RI.5.6 Analyze multiple accounts of the same event or topic, noting important similarities and differences in the point of view they represent.

Figure 2. CCSS for ELA/Literacy Informational Text—Craft and Structure (NGA & CCSSO, 2010, p. 14)

These functions are the business of school—they support all content learning. In order to ensure that students are learning the language of school, many teachers combine language forms and functions when teaching classroom academic language. Learning goals in a unit on the structure of the heart incorporating both form and function might include

- Ask-and-answer informational (wh- questions) and open-ended questions about the function and structure of the human heart with correct noun/verb agreement.

  Where does blood enter the heart? Blood enters the heart through _____.

  What do you know about the structure of the heart? The heart is _____.

- Tell the main idea of a text passage using a complex sentence.

  The main idea of the reading indicates that _____.

- Explain key details of a text passage using a descriptive sentence structure.

  The heart provides the body with food and oxygen in three ways: _____, _____, and _____.

In this chapter, we explore reading informational text in science, specifically the biology of the circulatory system and biographies of heart pioneers with ELLs in Grades 3–5. Scaffolding, learning sequence, reading informational text in depth, academic language skill integration, and the requirements of the CCSS for ELA/Literacy are important components of the instructional processes described here.

Rationale

Science is a content area that is particularly suited to what Bruner (1960) described as constructivist learning. An important concept in constructivism is that learning is an active process in which learners construct new ideas and concepts based upon the level of their current or past knowledge. Students engage in concrete experiences in which they discover principles by themselves. The teacher's role is to engage students in active dialogs and translate new information into a format appropriate to the learner's current state of understanding.

Bruner (1966) indicates that education must address (1) the child's predisposition to learning (motivation), (2) the ways in which learning can be structured so that it can be readily grasped by the learner (scaffolding), and (3) the sequence in which to present the material (concrete to abstract).

Bruner's theories (1960, 1966) have application to best practice for ELLs. The notion of scaffolding, for example, is of primary importance when teaching young language learners. Bruner first introduced the notion (Wood, Bruner, & Ross, 1976) and defined it as a type of support that teachers offer to learners. Scaffolding enables ELLs to engage in learning tasks even though they are not yet fully proficient in English. As students become more language proficient, teachers gradually remove the scaffolding, and learners begin to use tools and strategies for learning on their own. This gradual-release-of-responsibility model (Brown & Abell, 2007; Campione & Day, 1981; Fitzgerald & Graves, 2004; Levine & McCloskey, 2013) is supported by Bruner's theory of learning. Lessons begin with extensive teacher modeling and scaffolding, continue to a period of joint responsibility and guided practice, and result in full student responsibility for the application of learning. The model opens access to content-level information for students rather than excluding them, and is preferred for content learning for that reason.

The sequence of learning from concrete to abstract (Bruner, 1966) aligns itself neatly with the gradual-release-of-responsibility model. Students proceed from concrete experiences to ones that are increasingly abstract, from the known to the unknown. In science education, a model termed "the learning cycle" is based on decades of research that suggests that students learn better when they begin instructional sequences with concrete experiences, proceed to more scaffolded abstract learning through representations (such as reading), and then return to concrete experiences (Olson & Mokhtari, 2010; Brown & Abell, 2007; Lawson, 1995). For this reason, the learning cycle is a good model for structuring the learning of science concepts for ELLs.

The learning cycle stages are

1. *Exploration*: Students are presented with a guided experience involving concrete exploration or observation. They work to gather data on the phenomenon. It is critical for students to engage in exploration before teachers explain the phenomenon so that students can relate the new ideas to their own experiences and place them into a framework for understanding (Bransford, Brown, & Cocking, 2001). Interestingly, research has shown that vocabulary related to the exploration is better taught after the exploration phase (Brown & Abell, 2007). In this way, students can relate the new language and concepts with prior experiences.

2. *Concept development*: This phase enables students to interact orally with peers, texts, and teachers in an attempt to help students develop scientific concepts. It is carefully scaffolded. Teachers directly teach scientific vocabulary in this phase of the cycle and ask questions to enable learners to attach meaning to collected data. The data can then be assembled into charts or graphs and interpreted by students (Olson & Mokhtari, 2010).

3. *Application*: In this phase of the learning cycle, students use the science concepts in new ways—often in a more complex setting. They expand the application of learning beyond the initial exploration (Olson & Mokhtari, 2010). During this time, students work concretely but use their new ideas and scientific language while doing so.

Although the learning cycle was not designed for ELLs, it is very appropriate as a learning model. Concrete, "hands-on" exploration of scientific concepts provides ELLs with the communicatively meaningful social situations so critical to language learning and higher-level cognition (Vygotsky, 1962). Concrete learning experiences are understandable, even to children with few English language skills, and establishing an experiential basis for learning promotes conceptual development (Piaget & Inhelder, 1969). When teaching ELLs, a learning cycle model provides these essential hands-on experiences prior to dealing with in-depth reading of informational text. Activity-based, activities-oriented science instruction has been shown to encourage active engagement with scientific concepts and thus promote learning among ELLs (Lee, 2002; Lee & Fradd, 1996). In addition, August and Hakuta (1997) have noted the importance of specific instructional materials, appropriate to the needs of the students, to be an element of effective schooling for ELLs. This would include objects, models, and laboratory equipment relevant to the scientific topic.

The CCSS for ELA/Literacy suggest that teachers instruct students in close reading . This teaching technique is quite different from the experiential learning cycle procedures described earlier (Boyles, 2012). Close reading has been described as re-reading (Fisher, 2013)—requiring students to go back to the text repeatedly to respond to questions that require them to analyze text and understand what they are reading.

> Close, analytic reading stresses engaging with a text of sufficient complexity directly and examining its meaning thoroughly and methodically, encouraging students to read and reread deliberately. Directing student attention on the text itself empowers students to understand the central ideas and key supporting details. It also enables students to reflect on the meanings of individual words and sentences; the order in which sentences unfold; and the development of ideas over the course of the text, which ultimately leads students to arrive at an understanding of the text as a whole. (Partnership for Assessment of Readiness for College and Careers, 2012, p. 7)

For ELLs, dealing with complex text requires a classroom climate that promotes oral language interaction between and among teachers and students: a climate such as the one that results from experiential learning. Not surprisingly, a language development component in the science classroom has been shown to enhance ELLs' opportunities to learn and practice science discourse and writing (Minicucci, 1996). Students need to take in abundant amounts of targeted, scaffolded language as preparation for the close reading activities to follow. They will need opportunities to engage in extended periods of oral language discourse, perhaps while working collaboratively on hands-on science projects. Classrooms like these are collaborative—constructivist classrooms as described by Bruner (1960). Information is constructed among the learners—not delivered from the teacher. To be successful, teachers develop both content and language objectives for their students. They realize that ELLs do not acquire academic language but rather learn it as a result of a deliberate, planned, instructional process—a learning cycle—guided by language objectives. In this way, oral language learning precedes reading, occurs while reading, and follows reading of text.

In the description that follows, the educational practices described occur and reoccur in Grades 3–5. Instruction provides support for students with developing language skills and leads to higher level language development for dealing with text-based content learning.

Pedagogical Practice

Classrooms today consist of diverse student populations. Students come to the classroom with a variety of languages, skills, experiences, and interests. In order to teach all of these children effectively, teachers differentiate their instruction, choosing from a grade-level set of objectives, instructional techniques, materials, and assessments. The lessons described here offer suggestions for differentiating science lessons based on the circulatory system using informational texts (science texts about the biology of the system and biographies of heart scientists).

Overview

In the following lessons, students explore the human heart through experiential, hands-on learning and through close reading of informational text. The Pedagogy section is divided into two parts. In Part 1, the Learning Cycle, Grade 3 students learn the functions and structures of the heart in order to begin a unit on the circulatory system. In Part 2, Reading in Depth, students in Grades 4 and 5 read biographies of Charles Drew and Christian Barnard, famous heart scientists from the past.

The Learning Cycle Procedures

Instructional techniques commonly used in the three phases of the learning cycle (Exploration, Concept Development, and Application) are augmented with scaffolding procedures in order to help all learners comprehend the content. Each phase of the learning cycle contains several suggestions for scaffolding, promoting oral language, and instruction in reading strategies.

Exploration phase. Activation of prior knowledge at the beginning of the learning unit may be one of the most important ways that teachers can help learning to occur for ELLs. It has been said to be the "single most important factor influencing learning" (Ausubel, 1968). Activating students' prior learning of a topic makes them aware that they already know something about it. In addition, students become more cognitively engaged and focused on the new learning. Teachers also become aware of what students already know about the topic and can fill in learning gaps if they occur.

One simple technique for activating prior knowledge is to ask open-ended questions. Pairing students or assigning them to small groups to respond to an open-ended question such as *What do you know about the heart?* provides needed auditory input to ELLs in the group. As students report out on group information, there is another opportunity to hear the input and read it while the teacher writes the information, for example, on a whiteboard or chart. At this point, students can regroup and formulate questions that will help them to learn more about the heart and its functions.

After learning what students already know about the heart and the circulatory system, guided exploration of the topic in a concrete, hands-on situation allows students to explore the new concepts more fully. For this topic, teachers might pair students, providing each pair with a stethoscope. Teacher modeling will demonstrate the proper use of the instrument. While modeling, teachers have the opportunity to use the scientific language related to listening to the heart. Words such as *heartbeat, pulse, slow,* and *rapid* are appropriate.

Teacher modeling is also useful for demonstrating how students will collect data. For example, students can cycle through two of three listening phases, listening to heartbeats before and after exercise, to count the beats per minute. This data is collected on a graph or chart provided by the teacher. The activity can be further scaffolded if sentence frames are provided on the chart that can be used for oral reporting (e.g., *Before exercise, the heart beat at a rate of _____ beats per minute. After exercise, the heart beat at a rate of _____ beats per minute. I conclude that _____*). The sentence frames can then be used by students to create a written summary of the experiment in a learning journal.

Concept development phase. This phase of the lesson involves close reading of the text. An appropriate text for Grades 3–5 might be *The Heart: Our Circulatory System* by Seymour Simon (2006). This text uses scientific language and vocabulary to describe the circulatory system. It is highly attractive with colorful diagrams and photos taken with a scanning electron microscope. The reading level ranges into high Lexile levels (1120L), but the text is accessible to students from elementary to secondary grade levels because of the many photos and diagrams. Elementary students can learn from the visual information provided and from the short reading passages. Older learners will be scaffolded by the graphics while learning the correct terminology, scientific description, and latest technology for examining the circulatory system.

Engaging ELLs with text can begin with a picture walk through the text. A picture walk involves students, working in pairs, leafing through the text and examining the many pictures and diagrams. The teacher usually asks students to locate information related to a single topic, for example, *How is the heart constructed?* Pairing students for this phase of concept development will help ELLs to hear language related to the many pictures in the text. Student pairs can then report back to a larger group on what they have learned through looking at the pictures. Teachers can once again scaffold this language for ELLs: *I noticed that _____. I learned that _____. The picture on page XX shows that _____. I observed that _____.* Collecting the information on a chart reinforces the ideas that students collect in their small groups. The chart language can then be used later when students write summaries of their learning.

Close reading focuses on small sections of text, which are re-read for further information and increased comprehension. In *The Heart* (Simon, 2006), the teacher might focus on the full-page description of the location, the chambers, and the functions of the heart. Many teachers prefer to introduce new vocabulary at this point, before reading the text. Here, there are words that are primarily technical (*pump, chambers, septum, atria, atrium, ventricles, muscular, cell, valve*). There are also many academic terms in this text that are necessary for comprehension (*is divided, tilted, weighs, above, below, enters, upper, lower, heavier, stronger, right, left, one-way, backward*). Many of these words are clearly depicted in the drawings found opposite the text. Teachers can ask students to *listen and point* while calling out technical terms found in the drawing. Pairs of students can search for those pictured terms and point to them. The language input during listening activities such as these is valuable because students can immediately use the language to connect with the picture. The input becomes useful intake—language that is comprehended.

The academic terms in the text (*is divided, tilted, weighs, above, below, enters, upper, lower, right, left,* and *one-way*) can also be demonstrated with the use of the picture diagram and can be defined or demonstrated prior to reading.

Teachers approach the actual reading of the text for the first time in a variety of different ways. They choose a reading method that aligns with the reading and language proficiencies of their students. For low-level readers, teachers may choose to read aloud while students follow the print with a finger on the text. Also useful is partner reading. Students read simultaneously (useful when one student reads more fluently than the other) or take turns reading to each other. More proficient readers read individually and share the text information with a partner. Whatever method the teacher uses, reading is best comprehended when students are directed to read for a response to a question or in search of specific information: *How does blood flow into and out of the heart?*

The introduction of learning strategies related to reading is best accomplished within the content learning class. Learning strategies are important for all learners, to increase learning efficiency. But for ELLs, they are critical. ELLs are learning language and content simultaneously, a double burden. If teachers can help increase the efficiency of that task by teaching learning strategies, learning will accelerate for all students. Because the CCSS for ELA/Literacy for this lesson require students to "ask and answer questions," the question–answer relationships (QAR) strategy is appropriate for enabling ELLs to read for various types of specific information (Raphael, 1984).

For this strategy, the teacher prepares a list of questions on four levels: *right there questions, think and search questions, author and you questions,* and *on your own questions.* Right there questions are text-based and answered with one word or phrase. They may include *who . . . , what . . . , where . . . , how many . . . ,* and so on. Think and search questions are also text-based, but they require students to search across paragraphs or pages to find the answer. They may use words such as *summarize . . . , what causes . . . , how does . . . ,* and *retell. . . .* Think and search questions require students to respond in full sentences. Author and you questions require the reader to use prior knowledge to respond. These questions usually contain the word *you.* For example, *How are you aware that your heart is functioning?* On my own questions are also based on prior knowledge, but students need not read the text to respond to them. On my own questions usually ask students to write about a personal situation, problem, or event similar to the one in the reading (Levine, Lukens, & Smallwood, 2013). For the purpose of this lesson, the right there, think and search, and author and you questions satisfy the CCSS for ELA/Literacy.

The teacher models these three levels of questions around the text content and teaches students how to respond, perhaps using structured sentence frames. The students then work in small groups, asking and answering questions provided by the teacher. Next, students are asked to select the appropriate QAR category for each question and justify the choice in their small group. After practice in using this strategy with the text, the teacher may ask students to write their own QAR questions based on a new section of the text. Students ask each other their individual questions and exchange them with other groups who then must answer the questions, either orally or in writing (Levine et al., 2013). Through continued questioning, students are required to revisit the text many times. Each time, they have increased comprehension of the forms and functions of the language as well as the science content.

Assessment of reading comprehension can be accomplished through the QAR questions and responses. But there are other forms of assessment that promote further learning of the language and comprehension of the text. Many teachers ask students to integrate drawing into their learning experiences. Artistic expression incorporates multiple areas of the brain and motivates many reluctant readers. In this lesson, there is an opportunity for students to draw a diagram of the heart, labeling the various chambers, valves, and flows. Students can share their drawings with each other, and the teacher can post them in the classroom as an additional source of information.

Application phase. In the final phase of the learning cycle, students return to concrete application of the new concepts. In this phase, it is appropriate for teachers to require students to use the technical and academic vocabulary when speaking and writing. In order to provide a platform for language use, teachers may have students create a model of a heart. Teachers in the Teaching Learning Collaborative in California ask their Grade 5 students to use paper cups to create a model of the four chambers (Koehler, Martz, Montgomery, & Kinkaid, 2010). At the end of the project, each student creates a model heart and attaches it to the front of the chest. Students are now ready to present an oral summary of the function of the heart, its location in the body, and its connection to the circulatory system.

For ELLs, the teacher may scaffold the presentation with a graphic organizer citing the specifics of the summary and structuring the language forms to be used. Further scaffolding might include notecards for assistance in remembering terminology, and opportunities to practice the presentation. Another approach for the application phase, one taken by Donna, a special education teacher, is to obtain an animal heart as a focus for the presentation. Donna obtained the heart of a sheep, which is similar in size to a human heart. She scaffolded the information for her students so that they were able to proficiently describe the function of the heart. She then arranged to have her students visit other classrooms in the school, show the heart, and describe its functions. These students and their presentation were much in demand. They had many opportunities to use the language and learn the concepts.

Reading in Depth Procedures

The texts suggested here for Grades 4 and 5 are biographies of famous heart scientists. Additional accounts of the lives of the scientists can be found in encyclopedias or in web sources. These texts are excellent companions to the science instruction described earlier in the learning cycle on the nature of the heart and its relationship to the circulatory system. By combining both aspects of learning, teachers can teach needed reading strategies, promote reading in depth, and advance science concept development.

The procedures described at this point of the lesson involve close reading and re-reading of the text in depth. Because we are teaching ELLs, however, the approach we take to reading must be an integrated approach.

An Integrated Literacy Approach involves combining meaningful reading and writing, conversation with and about reading, and instruction in reading and writing skills and strategies used in authentic contexts. It meets the needs of a wide range of English language learners for developing literacy. A basic element is providing a print rich classroom in which students' oral language and literacy development are valued and put to use. (Levine & McCloskey, 2013, p. 179)

In this integrated approach to learning, many teachers of ELLs proceed using a three-part lesson structure: before, during, and after reading. The procedures for both Grades 4 and 5 can be described using this lesson structure.

Before. As in the learning cycle, we begin with activation of prior knowledge. The text used here for Grade 4 students is *Charles Drew: Doctor Who Got the World Pumped Up to Donate Blood* by Mike Venezia (2009). Most students will not be familiar with the subject of this biography, but they may be familiar with Drew's life work, the study of blood and plasma for use in transfusions. The lesson begins then with questions to small groups of students related to blood: *Why is blood essential for life? Why is it important to have a supply of blood for soldiers during wartime?* Students answer these questions using their prior learning and life experiences. Teachers scaffold their oral/written responses with sentence frames: *Blood is essential to life because blood provides the body with _____. During wartime, soldiers may require blood because _____.*

Other pre-reading activities that help students to use the language of biography involve sending students to web sites to find information about the topic. At one web site (Biography Channel,

2013) students find biographical information in shortened form. Using a structured outline format, students learn to note-take the following information:

Name: Charles Richard Drew

Occupation: doctor, surgeon

Birth Date: June 03, 1904

Death Date: April 01, 1950

Education: Amherst College, McGill University, Columbia University

Place of Birth: Washington, D.C.

Place of Death: Burlington, North Carolina

Using this information, students can create sentences about Dr. Drew such as

Charles Richard Drew was born on _____ in _____. He was a _____.

He was educated at _____, _____, and _____. He died on _____ in _____.

This short text will help students learn many of the language objectives for biography: vocabulary, verb forms, and sentence structure.

From here, students print out the short bio sketch on the web site to use as a first reading text. Having started with the outline format, much of this text will be familiar to students:

Charles Richard Drew was born on June 3, 1904, in Washington, D.C. He was an African-American physician who developed ways to process and store blood plasma in "blood banks." He directed the blood plasma programs of the United States and Great Britain in World War II, but resigned after a ruling that the blood of African-Americans would be segregated. He died in 1950. (Biography Channel, 2013)

The web site provides a photograph of Dr. Drew, a video showing and describing his major struggles, and a more complete biography. All of this information can be used to ask students "Tell me something I don't know about Dr. Charles Drew." ELLs take information from the web site to share orally. As the teacher goes around the room asking students to share information, students listen well so as not to repeat what another student has already said. At this time, students are taught to paraphrase, an important CCSS for ELA/Literacy skill. After one student has told a fact about Dr. Drew, the teacher calls on another student to "Tell me what _____ just said." Students need to hear utterances several times before they can adequately paraphrase. But eventually, paraphrasing becomes one of the skills used in a variety of contexts. At that point, students are better able to summarize and paraphrase sections of text.

During. A reading strategy that lends itself well to close reading is the directed reading/thinking activity (DRTA; Stauffer, 1969). DRTA is very useful in the *during* phase of the lesson. For this activity, the teacher groups students into small heterogeneous groups. The teacher models ways to preview the text, pointing out headers, pictures, graphs, or charts. The *Charles Drew* (Venezia, 2009) text is filled with many photographs, drawings, electron microscope scans, and cartoons. There is a glossary and an index at the end. The Lexile levels of this text range from 890 to 1060L, a range useful in late elementary and middle school. The text is very accessible to ELLs because of the many pictured elements and glosses of target vocabulary such as *blood bank*. This text preview therefore helps to provide students with a general summary of the topic.

Next, the teacher asks open-ended questions to encourage prediction of the content: *What do you predict that this text will be about?* Because of the work done in the *before* phase of the lesson, students will have some very good predictions. The teacher then directs students to read a short segment of the text. This can be done independently, with a partner, or through a teacher readaloud. The purpose is to help students confirm and refine their predictions. Students and teachers proceed in this manner through other sections of the text. Students summarize the content and are asked to go back to the text to find text passages that support their statements (Levine et al., 2013). DRTA helps students to learn several important reading strategies: previewing, prediction, verification of predictions with text citations, and summarization.

After. After reading, students compare the text to information located in an encyclopedia or on the web site. This is a standard required in Grade 4 (RI.4.6) when students learn to compare information found in two texts. To help with this comparison, a chart is useful (see Figure 3). Here, students note-take information found from two separate sources and decide if it is the same or different. To promote reporting and writing about these similarities and differences, teachers model the use of the signal words (*however, both*) and provide sentence frames to help students create comparisons. Signal words are part of the academic language that ELLs must acquire to be able to read academic text with comprehension. When comparing and contrasting texts, sentences such as the following are common:

The web site defines plasma as _____. However, the text defines plasma as _____.

Both texts indicate that _____.

The procedures described here also apply to Grade 5 reading of informational text. At this grade, students may be asked to read a biography of Christian Barnard, another famous surgeon,

	Biography of Charles Drew (Biography Channel, 2013)	*Charles Drew: Doctor Who Got the World Pumped Up to Donate Blood* (Venezia, 2009)
How does the text define blood plasma?		
What does the text tell about the differences between plasma and whole blood?		
What does the text tell us about why plasma is better for blood transfusions?		
What does the text say was Dr. Drew's greatest accomplishment regarding blood plasma?		

Figure 3. Information Provided in Two Texts About Charles Drew

one noted for attempting the first heart transplant. Using techniques similar to those used with the *Charles Drew* (Venezia, 2009) text, teachers uncover what students already know about the topic, search for web-based information, search the library for information, report using oral sentence frames, and eventually write short summaries. Comparison charts can be used to compare Dr. Barnard to Dr. Drew—both men left their countries and immigrated elsewhere to get an education, and both men made outstanding contributions to medicine—particularly related to the heart and the uses for blood for transfusions. In addition, both men had to fight popular prejudices in order to be successful. ELLs may find that these physician models have something to teach them about perseverance for a personal goal.

CCSS for ELA/Literacy RI.5.6 requires that Grade 5 students analyze an author's point of view. The *Charles Drew* (Venezia, 2009) text allows students to analyze the language of the text to determine viewpoint. Once again, charts are helpful for structuring this learning. Figure 4 organizes language and questions for this analysis. In order to scaffold the learning, students get social support from working in small groups or pairs. They profit from extensive oral language support, such as sentence frames, in order to share or report on their conclusions from the text analysis. Teachers model the appropriate academic language, focusing on the language objectives for the lesson, for example, *The author used the word "unfortunately" because he felt* _____. *The author indicates that he opposes prejudice when he writes* _____. Eventually, the oral language and graphic supports will enable students to write acceptable analysis paragraphs that conform to the CCSS for ELA/Literacy.

Reflection Questions and Action Plans

Diverse learners may require modifications of a lesson in order to achieve the Common Core Standards guiding classroom instruction through the use of rigorous informational texts. Teachers have many ways in which to support language learners and to provide challenge to high achieving students.

Questions About the Text	Quotations From the Text	Your Ideas About the Text
1. Why does the writer begin the sentence with the word "unfortunately"? 2. What does the phrase "he suffered" tell you about how Dr. Drew felt? 3. Does the author believe the military was "prejudiced"? How do you know?	Unfortunately, while Dr. Drew was setting up the program, he suffered one of the greatest disappointments of his life. He learned that the U.S. military had decided not to accept blood donations from African Americans. Because of the Army's prejudice, even Dr. Drew was unable to donate blood!	1. 2. 3.

Figure 4. Point of View—Charles Drew: Doctor Who Got the World Pumped Up to Donate Blood (Venezia, 2009)

Reflect on the following practices (Levine & McCloskey, 2013) and decide in what ways they can help both groups of learners be successful:

- Develop activities to activate prior learning in preparation for reading classroom texts. Guide students in ways to structure their oral language responses.

- Help learners to create and use a reading journal.

- Create, or ask students to create, oral language dialogues related to classroom texts. Record these on YouTube.

- Use graphic organizers to summarize classroom readings, for example, a timeline for a biography text.

- Develop point of view by asking students to write questions to ask the characters in the reading.

- Teach small groups of learners how to ask questions about a text: details, clarification, prediction, and summary. Pair learners to ask questions of each other.

- Reflect on why it is important to help students develop academic competence in aural/oral language in order to achieve at a high level in reading informational text.

Action research is one way that teachers help themselves to grow professionally. Reflect on the following ideas for action research. Choose one and conduct research in your classroom:

- What methods do I use to teach vocabulary? How can I increase my instructional techniques for vocabulary learning?

- What reading strategies have I taught my students? What other strategies can I incorporate into my teaching to help a wide range of learners?

- How do I check student comprehension of a text? Am I checking the comprehension of all learners in my classroom? Are my techniques successful? What other ways can I check on reading comprehension?

Suggested Activities

- Re-read this chapter and list the many ways that teachers scaffold a complex text for students in Grades 3–5. Begin to integrate these practices, when appropriate, into your classroom instruction.

- Design a lesson for social studies that is based on the same CCSS for ELA/Literacy found in this lesson. Create a range of activities for the many diverse learners in your classroom.

8

Helping ELLs Read and Write to Grade-Level Text

Diane August and Erin F. Haynes, American Institutes for Research

The CCSSs and Specific Demands for ELLs

The Common Core State Standards for English Language Arts and Literacy in History/Social Studies, Science, and Technical Subjects (CCSS for ELA/Literacy; National Governors Association Center for Best Practices [NGA] & Council of Chief State School Officers [CCSSO], 2010a), adopted by 45 states, the District of Columbia, and four territories, reflects the knowledge and skills that all students, including ELLs, need for success in college and careers. These new standards, while challenging, provide an exciting opportunity to create methods and materials that will assist ELLs in acquiring grade-level skills and knowledge. This chapter presents a research-based approach, Augmented Curriculum for ELLs (ACE), to help ELLs meet the standards, specifically focused on the Grade 4 ELA standards for narrative texts. A portion of the Grade 4 narrative text that we draw on as an example, Frances Hodgson Burnett's *The Secret Garden* (1911), is presented in Figure 1.[1]

A number of standards are always met through the ACE approach, no matter what the text, and other standards can be met through ACE depending on the selected text. Table 1 presents Grade 4 ELA standards that are applicable to most texts using the ACE approach in the left-hand column (e.g., Engage effectively in a range of collaborative discussions). The right-hand column includes standards that are not met through every text, but that are particularly applicable to our example text, *The Secret Garden* (Burnett, 1911).

---

[1] The full text is available as part of Project Gutenberg at http://www.gutenberg.org/ebooks/113.

When Mary Lennox was sent to Misselthwaite Manor to live with her uncle everybody said she was the most disagreeable-looking child ever seen. It was true, too. She had a little thin face and a little thin body, thin light hair and a sour expression. Her hair was yellow, and her face was yellow because she had been born in India and had always been ill in one way or another. Her father had held a position under the English Government and had always been busy and ill himself, and her mother had been a great beauty who cared only to go to parties and amuse herself with gay people. She had not wanted a little girl at all, and when Mary was born she handed her over to the care of an Ayah, who was made to understand that if she wished to please the Mem Sahib she must keep the child out of sight as much as possible. So when she was a sickly, fretful, ugly little baby she was kept out of the way, and when she became a sickly, fretful, toddling thing she was kept out of the way also. She never remembered seeing familiarly anything but the dark faces of her Ayah and the other native servants, and as they always obeyed her and gave her her own way in everything, because the Mem Sahib would be angry if she was disturbed by her crying, by the time she was six years old she was as tyrannical and selfish a little pig as ever lived. The young English governess who came to teach her to read and write disliked her so much that she gave up her place in three months, and when other governesses came to try to fill it they always went away in a shorter time than the first one. So if Mary had not chosen to really want to know how to read books she would never have learned her letters at all.

Figure 1. Excerpt From Frances Hodgson Burnett's The Secret Garden *(1911, pp. 1–2)*

The standards presented in Table 1 pose challenges to all students, English proficient and ELLs alike, at the word, sentence, and text levels. However, there are additional challenges for ELLs. Challenges for all students at the word level include words with multiple meanings, nominalization,[2] unfamiliar vocabulary, and use of language that is archaic (see Fisher, Frey, & Lapp, 2012). For example, in *The Secret Garden* (Burnett, 1911), students may have difficulty with multimeaning words like *light* in "thin light hair" or *sour* in "sour expression," and with unfamiliar words like *manor*. For ELLs, an added challenge at the word level is that many more of the content words in a given text are unfamiliar, greatly reducing comprehension. Complex connectives, such as those introducing subordinate clauses and phrases (e.g., *when, which*), pose an additional challenge (Snow & Uccelli, 2009).

At the sentence level, all students are challenged by sophisticated use of figurative language (Fisher, Frey, & Lapp, 2012). Nonstandard dialects of English can also be difficult. For example, in *The Secret Garden* (Burnett, 1911), some of the dialogue is presented in Yorkshire English, as when the station-master speaks to the servant who has picked up Mary: "'I see tha's got back,' he said. 'An' tha's browt th' young 'un with thee'" (p. 19). ELLs are further challenged by complex syntax characterized by compound sentences with two or more independent clauses or an independent clause and dependent clauses. The first paragraph of *The Secret Garden* includes several complex sentences, including the following:

The young English governess who came to teach her to read and write disliked her so much that she gave up her place in three months, and when other governesses came to try to fill it they always went away in a shorter time than the first one. (Burnett, 1911, p. 2)

---

[2] Nominalization is the conversion of verbs, adjectives, or adverbs into nouns (e.g., *express* → *expression*).

Table 1. Grade 4 CCSS for ELA/Literacy Standards Applicable to Most Texts Through ACE, and Standards Applicable Specifically to *The Secret Garden*

Standards Applicable to Most Texts	Standards Applicable to *The Secret Garden*
Reading: Literature	
RL.4.1 Refer to details and examples in a text when explaining what the text says explicitly and when drawing inferences from the text.	**RL.4.2** Determine a theme of a story, drama, or poem from details in the text; summarize the text.
RL.4.4 Determine the meaning of words and phrases as they are used in a text, including those that allude to significant characters found in mythology.	**RL.4.3** Describe in depth a character, setting, or event in a story or drama, drawing on specific details in the text (e.g., a character's thoughts, words, or actions).
RL.4.10 By the end of the year, read and comprehend literature, including stories, dramas, and poetry, in the Grades 4–5 text complexity band proficiently, with scaffolding as needed at the high end of the range.	
Writing	
W.4.4 Produce clear and coherent writing in which the development, organization, and style are appropriate to task, purpose, and audience.	**W.4.2** Write informative/explanatory texts to examine a topic and convey ideas and information clearly.
W.4.9 Draw evidence from literary or informational texts to support analysis, reflection, and research.	
Speaking and Listening	
SL.4.1 Engage effectively in a range of collaborative discussions (one-on-one, in groups, and teacher-led) with diverse partners on Grade 4 topics and texts, building on others' ideas and expressing their own clearly.	
SL.4.3 Identify the reasons and evidence a speaker provides to support particular points.	
Language	
L.4.1 Demonstrate command of the conventions of standard English grammar and usage when writing or speaking.	**L.4.5b** Recognize and explain the meaning of common idioms, adages, and proverbs.
L.4.2 Demonstrate command of the conventions of standard English capitalization, punctuation, and spelling when writing.	
L.4.4 Determine or clarify the meaning of unknown and multiple-meaning words and phrases based on Grade 4 reading and content, choosing flexibly from a range of strategies.	

This sentence contains three dependent clauses (*who came to teach her, that she gave up her place,* and *when other governesses came*) and two independent clauses (*The young governess . . . disliked her so much* and *they always went away . . .*), making it a difficult sentence for ELLs.

Finally, at the text level, all students may be challenged by distortions in organization of time (e.g., flashbacks or foreshadowing), limited use of text features and graphics, text with multiple levels of meaning, and assumed specialized content knowledge (Fisher, Frey, & Lapp, 2012). They must also grapple with understanding the structures and purposes that underlie the different rhetorical modes, including exposition, argumentation, description, and narration. In addition to these challenges, English poses a particular challenge to ELLs in its use of reference chains (see Uccelli, 2012), where the same people or things are linked throughout a text using pronouns (e.g., *he, they, it*) or the same concepts are linked using multiple expressions. For example, in the first sentence of *The Secret Garden* (Burnett, 1911), there are multiple references to Mary (marked with underlining): "When <u>Mary Lennox</u> was sent to Misselthwaite Manor to live with <u>her</u> uncle everybody said <u>she</u> was the most disagreeable-looking child ever seen . . ." (p. 1). Later in the paragraph, reference is made to Mary (marked with underlining) as well as her mother (marked with italics) in the same sentence: "<u>Her</u> *mother* had been a great beauty *who* cared only to go to parties" (p. 1).

The ACE approach provides linguistic support specific to these challenges, thus assisting all students, including ELLs, in meeting grade-level standards. The next section provides rationale for the methods used in ACE that target challenges at the word, sentence, and text level described above.

Rationale

One major challenge that ELLs face, and for which they require additional support to meet the CCSS for ELA/Literacy, is in vocabulary acquisition. According to research by Nation (1990), students need to understand approximately 95% of the words in a text to comprehend it. However, ELLs tend to have much smaller English vocabularies than their English-proficient peers (Mancilla-Martinez & Lesaux, 2010). Using the ACE approach, teachers identify words that are frequent in English texts at the target grade level and those that are important for understanding the text. Because it is not tenable to teach students every unfamiliar word in a text, the ACE approach focuses more intensive vocabulary instruction (extended instruction) on words that are abstract, as these are harder for students to acquire (August, Artzi, Barr, & Massoud, 2013). Embedded instruction is less intensive and is provided for more concrete and less frequent words; our research (August, Barr, Artzi, & Massoud, 2013) shows that both types of instruction, when properly executed, are effective in helping ELLs acquire vocabulary.

The CCSS for ELA/Literacy also requires students to use strategies to determine the meanings of unknown words (L.4.4). The ACE approach therefore includes mini-lessons on word learning strategies such as using context clues, word morphology, and reference guides (e.g., online dictionaries) to help students acquire words on their own. It also teaches ELLs who speak languages that share cognates with English, such as Spanish and Portuguese, to use cognate knowledge to determine the meanings of unknown English words. Some ELLs may not utilize their cognate knowledge without explicit instruction in how to do so (Nagy, Garcia, Durgunoglu, & Hancin-Bhatt, 1993).

Another major challenge for ELLs is complex syntax. It is helpful for teachers to recognize and understand the grammatical demands associated with texts in their discipline and to show students how different grammatical choices affect meaning (Schleppegrell, Achugar, & Oteíza, 2004). Gaining this understanding is critical for ELLs both in terms of their comprehension and their writing (e.g., W.4.4). The ACE approach guides students through complex portions of text using an adaptation of the method of linguistic analysis used by Schleppegrell and de Oliveira (2013).

At the level of the whole text, ELLs may lack specialized content knowledge, including historical and cultural knowledge that may be known by their native-English-speaking peers.[3] This knowledge can be critical to drawing inferences from the text as required by standards RL.4.1 and W.4.9. For example, it is helpful to understand the role of Britain in India to draw inferences about Mary and her family in *The Secret Garden* (Burnett, 1911). In the ACE approach, teachers determine areas of the text for which specialized background knowledge is required but may be lacking and provide short lessons to students to fill in this knowledge before they read the target text. Some background information is presented through additional text, but carefully chosen pictures, video clips, maps, diagrams, and other such media are also used. Background lessons that use text and the target text itself are presented through an interactive reading process in which students answer text-based questions and provide evidence for their answers from the text (RL.4.1 and SL.4.3). To help ELLs answer difficult grade-level questions, they are asked supplemental questions. By answering the additional questions, students incrementally develop a better understanding of the text.

The ACE approach incorporates techniques to support ELLs across the word, sentence, and text levels because research indicates that ELLs benefit from additional support when learning English and content concurrently (August & Shanahan, 2006). Examples of techniques from language arts include creating opportunities for children to act out meanings of words and passages, and using visual aids to illustrate the meanings of words and phrases in authentic contexts (Silverman, 2007); creating opportunities for teacher–student interaction around books to increase comprehension during reading (Koskinen et al., 2000); and engaging students in collaborative discussion to guide meaning-oriented responses to text content (Saunders & Goldenberg, 2010).

The ACE approach uses these supports and others, including graphic organizers, sentence frames, paragraph frames, and word banks, all tailored to students' proficiency levels, to help ELLs meet grade-level standards in language and writing (e.g., W.4.4, L.4.1–2). Structured opportunities for interaction with peers and the teacher are also an important part of the ACE approach because research shows that these types of interactions help ELLs acquire both language and content knowledge faster (Gersten et al., 2007; Mackey & Goo, 2007; Swain, 2000; Genesee, Lindholm-Leary, Saunders, & Christian, 2005), and because they are part of standard SL.4.1.

Pedagogical Practice: Augmented Curriculum for ELLs

The Augmented Curriculum for ELLs (ACE) approach supplements grade-level curricula and instructional methods to provide support to ELLs at different proficiency levels.[4] Table 2 provides an overview of one possible format of an ACE unit. In this three-lesson unit there are two mainstream lessons that include additional supports for ELLs, preceded by a lesson that prepares ELLs

---

[3] Conversely, ELLs may have knowledge from their own cultures that native English speakers do not have; it is important to draw on students' background knowledge and incorporate their cultural perspectives into classroom activities (see Park & King, 2003), a practice that can enrich instruction for all students (Gonzalez, Moll, & Amanti, 2005).

[4] All examples are provided at the Emergent level; differentiation techniques are described in the following section.

Table 2. Example of Format for a Mainstream Unit Augmented for ELLs

Lesson	Description	Support for ELLs	Provider
1	ELL supplementary lesson	• Background (historical or cultural) information • Interactive reading of the first section of text — Embedded and extended vocabulary instruction — Text-based questions focused on comprehension — Individual or paired students identify unknown vocabulary or confusing sections of the passage • Analysis of grammar • Summary of the text	Mainstream classroom teacher/ESL specialist
2	Mainstream lesson	• Mini-lesson on text features (e.g., idioms) or word-learning skills (e.g., cognates) • Interactive reading of the first section of text, with a focus on mainstream text analysis (*use additional comprehension questions, answer frames, and word banks as appropriate*)	Mainstream classroom teacher
3	Mainstream lesson	• Scaffolded mainstream essay (*use supplementary questions, graphic organizers, paragraph frames, and word banks as appropriate*) • Assessment	Mainstream classroom teacher

for the mainstream lessons.[5] Each lesson takes approximately 45 minutes. In the following sections, we describe factors to consider in selecting appropriate text for the unit, methods to support ELLs during the mainstream lessons, and supplementary support for ELLs, which in this model is provided during lessons that take place prior to the mainstream lessons.

Selecting Appropriate Text

Texts should be selected based on quantitative and qualitative measures, as well as reader and task considerations (NGA & CCSSO, 2010b). The Lexile system is one popular framework for determining quantitative difficulty; the Lexile "Find a Book" site allows users to search for books (mostly narrative texts) at different difficulty levels.[6] Other options for finding books at different levels include the Accelerated Reader,[7] which uses the ATOS Book Level and the Questar Degree of Reading Power (DRP) Analyzer.[8]

Qualitative measures are more subjective, and include the levels of meaning or purpose of the text, its structure, and clarity of language; required background knowledge (NGA & CCSSO,

---

[5] It may be necessary to present the text in chunks over additional days. In this case, provide preparation lessons for each portion of the text, followed by the scaffolded mainstream lesson for that portion.

[6] http://lexile.com/findabook

[7] http://www.arbookfind.com/

[8] http://www.questarai.com/products/drpprogram/pages/textbook_readability.aspx

---

2010b, p. 5); as well as the measures of text complexity, as described in the first section of this chapter. Consider the factors that may make text particularly challenging for ELLs (e.g., additional unfamiliar words, complex syntax, reference chains). Other important factors to consider in selecting text relate to the task and reader. The text should be appropriate for the tasks at hand and should take into consideration reader factors such as interest.

Note that whereas ELLs need to read and analyze grade-level text, they should also be involved in reading large amounts of text at levels that enable more independent reading. Wide reading is crucially important for ELLs because much background knowledge (and the vocabulary that indexes it) is acquired in this way (August & Shanahan, 2010).

The text used in this chapter, *The Secret Garden* (Burnett, 1911), has a Lexile level of 970L, which is in the Grade 4–5 stretch band. Qualitatively, it features some use of archaic and unfamiliar vocabulary, as well as some dialogue in a nonstandard dialect of English. Its primary challenge for ELLs lies in its extensive use of reference chains. It is used as the example text here because it is one of the CCSS for ELA/Literacy Grade 4–5 Text Exemplars (NGA & CCSSO, 2010c).

Support During the Mainstream Lesson

The CCSS for ELA/Literacy represents key shifts in instruction, with an increased focus on reading text closely and text-based evidence, writing from sources, and using academic vocabulary. ACE provides support to ELLs around each of these areas.

Reading Text Closely and Text-Based Evidence

The CCSS for ELA/Literacy makes reading text closely a central focus of instruction. Close reading is the practice of reading text carefully with a focus on the author's meaning rather than the reader's personal reactions. Students receive guidance through sequences of thought-provoking, text-dependent questions that encourage them to examine textual evidence and discern deep meaning (Achieve, 2014). For ELLs, we suggest using interactive reading techniques and conducting more than one reading of a text. Whereas we describe one method of structuring this interactive reading with ELLs below, there are many different ways to engage students with text. Methods will differ depending on the classroom composition, the text, and the number and type of instructors available to support ELLs.

Using the ACE approach, the teacher first reads the text out loud to give students a feel for how it sounds when read by a fluent speaker. The teacher embeds vocabulary instruction during this reading by pausing briefly to explain difficult words or asking students to define them by drawing on content knowledge, cognate knowledge, and context. Prior to a second reading, the teacher provides extended instruction for key vocabulary words that are abstract. During the second reading, he or she poses a series of text-dependent questions that are focused on key ideas and details. These questions are meant to assist students in answering the more challenging questions in the mainstream lesson. This kind of questioning will help build students' confidence by starting small (e.g., *Who took care of Mary? What was she told to do?*). The questions also target vocabulary (e.g., *What does "make to understand" mean? What were the servants made to understand about the baby?*), identify key ideas (e.g., *How did Mary behave?*), and disentangle meaning in complex sections of text.

In a third reading of the text, students are asked more challenging text-dependent questions that align with more challenging main idea and detail standards (e.g., *List all the evidence from the first paragraph about Mary's appearance. Why does the narrator tell the reader the description is "true?"* [RL.4.3]) as well as with craft and structure and integration of knowledge and ideas standards.

Depending on their proficiency level, students may do the second and third readings as a whole class, with a partner, or individually, with ongoing teacher support. At any point after the second reading, students might be asked to identify words they still don't know and questions they still might have, noting these in a journal. Students can then use strategies they have learned (including dictionary use) to find the meanings of words they still don't know and add the definitions to their journal entries. They may define unfamiliar words for classmates and select some of these words for posting on a word wall. Students can debrief as a class and help each other with the questions they still have about the text. During the readings, scaffolds such as sentence frames and word banks can help students with more limited proficiency in English answer questions. These scaffolds should be tailored to students' levels of proficiency. Figure 2 provides an example.

Writing From Sources

The CCSS for ELA/Literacy calls for clear and coherent writing from sources in a variety of rhetorical modes (exposition, argument, or narrative) in which students draw information from text (Tri-State Collaborative, 2012). In the ACE approach, scaffolding to assist ELLs in writing includes supplemental questions to help students better understand the essay prompt. For example, for the expository essay prompt, *What can the reader infer from the text about how to avoid falling ill from*

1. Who was Mary's Ayah?

   Mary's Ayah was a _____ who took care of Mary.

2. Why did the Ayah take care of Mary?

   Mary's mother _____ (did/did not) want Mary.

3. What did Mary's mother tell the Ayah to do?

   She told the Ayah to keep Mary _____ and _____.

4. Why did the Ayah and other servants always obey Mary?

   Mary's mother would be angry if she heard Mary _____.

5. The servants always obeyed Mary. As a consequence, or result, how did Mary behave?

   Mary was a _____ and _____ little pig.

Word Bank		
crying	quiet	servant
out of site	selfish	tyrannical

Figure 2. Supplemental Questions and Answer Frames

cholera?, a scaffolded prompt might state, *In the story, Mary's Ayah and many other people die from a disease called cholera. Based on what people in the story do and say, what can we infer, or guess, about how you can keep from getting cholera?* Other scaffolding techniques include providing graphic organizers, word banks, and paragraph frames. Paragraph frames are particularly important to help ELLs learn how to construct the various types of writing required by the CCSS for ELA/Literacy. In elementary school, student writing should be approximately 30% argumentative, 35% informative or explanatory, and 35% narrative (NGA & CCSSO, 2010b). For example, an expository paragraph frame might include space for an introduction (e.g., *State the problem*), a summary of evidence from the text (e.g., *State what happened*), students' interpretation or inferences (e.g., *Write what you learned*), and a conclusion. The graphic organizer would assist students in finding these pieces of information in the text before they start writing. Students can work in pairs or groups to fill out the graphic organizer, then work individually on their paragraphs.

Academic Vocabulary

The standards call for focusing on general academic and domain-specific vocabulary in context throughout instruction (Tri-State Collaborative, 2012). As discussed above, it is especially critical to build ELLs' vocabulary throughout instruction. With the ACE approach, direct vocabulary instruction is done in two ways: through extended instruction, which consists of providing definitions and contextual information, involving students in discussing words, and reviewing the words in various contexts (Graves, August, & Mancilla-Martinez, 2012); and through embedded instruction, in which students quickly learn word definitions as they encounter the words in text (August, Artzi, Barr, & Massoud, 2013).

Both general academic and domain-specific words should be selected based on frequency in English texts and unfamiliarity to students. For elementary grades, the First 4000 Words Project is a good resource for highly frequent words.[9] Another criterion for selecting words is their importance for understanding the text at hand.

Because students acquire abstract words less easily than other types of words, we recommend selecting two or three of the most abstract words each day for extended instruction.[10] An abstract word is one that is not easily imageable, or one that requires great effort to form an image in your mind. Examples of words that are easily imageable are *dinosaur, pencil,* and *rain*. Examples of words that are not easily imageable (and therefore candidates for extended instruction) are *spirit, promise,* and *merely*. Other features of abstract words are concreteness and relatedness. A word is concrete if it refers to something tangible, that is, if it refers to something that can be easily felt, smelled, seen, heard, or tasted (e.g., *bacon*). Examples of nonconcrete, abstract words are *era, expensive,* and *indeed*. Relatedness is the degree to which understanding the word requires an understanding of related concepts. Words that can be understood in isolation from other terms and concepts are unrelated (and not abstract), but words that require a great deal of background knowledge on a given topic have a high degree of relatedness. An example of a word with low relatedness is *lion*,

---

[9] http://www.sewardreadingresources.com/fourkw.html

[10] Both general academic and domain-specific words can be abstract or concrete; abstractness cuts across categories, but is an important consideration in selecting words.

which requires only some knowledge about animals. A word with high relatedness is *economy*, because it is related to dozens of other concepts.

Examples of highly frequent, abstract words in the first section of *The Secret Garden* (Burnett, 1911) are *true, expression, position,* and *government.* These words would be instructed using extended instruction techniques. (However, for ELLs who can draw on first-language cognate knowledge, these words can be taught through embedded instructional techniques.) The ACE method of extended instruction consists of defining the word in context, presenting a picture and talking about how the picture illustrates the word, and providing a short turn and talk activity that students can do with a partner. Generally, the turn and talks give students an opportunity to talk about some aspect of the word that relates it to their own experiences or knowledge. See Figure 3 for an example. This example also provides a definition in Spanish, drawing on ELLs' first language knowledge, and asks students to determine the word's cognate status. It additionally asks students to spell the word.

All other words selected for instruction, including highly frequent, concrete words and words important for understanding the text, can be taught using embedded instruction techniques. Embedded instruction occurs throughout the lesson, whenever the target words are encountered. The teacher may provide a definition or explanation, or may ask students to define the word by drawing on background knowledge or using cognate knowledge, context clues, or reference guides. Teachers may also provide students with a glossary of words in the text—for glossaries, it is important to use child-friendly definitions such as those found at wordsmyth.net.

Students see:

The teacher says:
Expression means what your face looks like to show how you feel inside. Look at the illustration. This girl is angry. She has a sour expression, like Mary. Everybody make a sour expression.

Expression in Spanish is *expresión.* Is expression a cognate? [yes]

Partner talk. What is something that would make you have a sour expression?

Let's spell expression. [e,x,p,r,e,s,s,i,o,n] What word have we spelled? [*expression*]

Figure 3. Word Card for Extended Instruction of Expression

Integrating Additional Supports

In addition to support provided during a mainstream lesson, it is useful to provide ELLs with additional information and instruction to enhance their comprehension and, ultimately, their ability to meet the CCSS for ELA/Literacy. Building background knowledge is important both in skills required by the language arts lesson and in terms of content or cultural knowledge necessary to understand a particular text. For language arts skills, ELLs benefit from mini-lessons related to vocabulary acquisition (e.g., using cognates, context clues, morphology, and reference guides to determine the meanings of unknown words). These are skills that are required by the substandards in L.4.4. ELLs also benefit from instruction related to grade-level text features targeted by the CCSS for ELA/Literacy. For example, substandards in L.4.5 require students to understand and explain similes, metaphors, common idioms, and proverbs. Particular texts lend themselves better to some mini-lessons than others. For example, there are many idioms in the *The Secret Garden* (Burnett, 1911); the first paragraph alone includes several, including "held a position," "her own way," "gave up her place," and "learned her letters" (p. 1).

ELLs also benefit from learning background information about the text at hand. For example, *The Secret Garden* (Burnett, 1911) is difficult to understand without some knowledge of its historical and cultural context, including, for example, knowledge about the role of Great Britain in India, and cholera (the disease that kills Mary's parents). Here are some example activities to build students' background knowledge before reading *The Secret Garden*.

- Looking at a world map to see where England and India are.

- Reading about the English in India to find out why they were there, and what life in India was like before India won independence from England.

- Watching a short video clip about cholera.

Background knowledge activities can be created or adapted from a variety of sources. In the ACE approach, the activities are very brief—students don't need to become experts, but they do need to understand enough about the topic to comprehend the text. Background knowledge activities should not reveal the meaning of the text students are preparing to read, but rather supplement it. Finally, as with the text, it is important to scaffold the background activities with embedded vocabulary instruction, questions, answer frames, and word banks as appropriate.

In addition to background knowledge, ELLs may require support in understanding the syntax in a text, especially for texts with a large number of complex sentences (as in *The Secret Garden*, Burnett, 1911). After the interactive reading, the ACE approach guides students through complex sentences using an adaptation of the linguistic analysis described by Schleppegrell and Achugar (2003) and Schleppegrell and de Oliveira (2013). See Figure 4 for an example.

First (Part A in Figure 4), students identify the actor in the sentence, or who did the action (*the young English governess*). Then they identify the action (*disliked*) and the recipient of the action (*her,* i.e., *Mary*). Next, they fill in descriptive details (e.g., *who came to teach her to read and write* describes the governess). Breaking apart complex sentences in this way allows students to arrive at the key elements of the sentence. Second (Part B), they rewrite each element of the sentence in

(A)	The young English governess who came to teach her to read and write disliked her so much that she gave up her place in three months.
	Who (Actor): *The young English governess* 　Descriptor (Detail): *who came to teach her to read and write* What Happened (Action): *disliked* What (Recipient): *her* 　　Descriptor (Detail): *so much* 　　　Descriptor (Detail): *that she gave up her place in three months*

(B)	Sentence Element	*The Secret Garden*	Say It In Your Own Words
	Who	The young English governess	*the teacher from England*
	Descriptor	who came to teach her to read and write	*the teacher was supposed to teach Mary reading and writing*
	What Happened	disliked	didn't like
	What	her	*Mary*
	Descriptor	so much	*so much*
	Descriptor	that she gave up her place in three months	*that she quit her job in three months*

(C)	Write the sentence from *The Secret Garden* in your own words. (Use the sentence elements to guide you.)		
	Who?	*What happened?*	*What?*
	The teacher from England didn't like Mary.		
	Descriptor (detail)		
	The teacher was supposed to teach Mary reading and writing.		
	Descriptor (Detail)		
	She quit her job in three months.		

Figure 4. Linguistic Analysis of a Complex Sentence From The Secret Garden *(Burnett, 1911)*

their own words, and third (Part C), they reconstruct the complex sentence. Teaching students this skill will help them navigate other complex sentences that they encounter.

Assessment

The final aspect of the ACE approach is formative assessment to ensure that students understand and can analyze the text. One form of assessment is having students write a short summary of the text to ensure that they understand what they have read. This activity can be scaffolded for ELLs at different levels of proficiency through summary paragraph frames and word banks. Another form of assessment is having students independently answer text-dependent questions of varying levels of difficulty from the interactive readings. Prior to answering questions independently, ELLs may benefit from instruction that clarifies the task demands of particular question types as well as construct-irrelevant vocabulary associated with the question. Questions used for assessing students should be aligned to the CCSS for ELA/Literacy. Table 3 provides an example.

Table 3. CCSS for ELA/Literacy-Aligned Questions and Supports for ELLs

Question	Standard	Additional Support for ELLs
The story says that Mary had a sour expression. What does sour expression mean, and what does it tell us about Mary?	RL.4.4 Determine the meaning of words and phrases.	How to provide a complete answer to a two-part question
Why did the Ayah, rather than Mary's mother, take care of Mary?	RL.4.3 Describe an event in a story.	What *rather than* means
Why is Mary such a disagreeable little girl to everyone?	RL.4.2 Determine a theme of a story.	How to respond when the question word is *why*

Differentiating Instruction

The ACE approach differentiates instruction to take into account students' levels of proficiency and prior schooling experiences. For example, during interactive reading, both sentence frames and a word bank can be provided to emergent ELLs; for intermediate ELLs, reduced frames may be sufficient; and advanced ELLs may only need a word bank or no support at all. In heterogeneous classes, more advanced ELLs or English-proficient students can be paired with ELLs at lower proficiency levels to read or write, or the teacher might work with emergent-level ELLs while students at intermediate and advanced proficiency levels work in pairs or individually. The whole class can then be regrouped to discuss each task.

This section has provided a number of descriptions and examples to meet the CCSS for ELA/Literacy with ELLs. Table 4 provides a summary of the activities and strategies, along with the standards that they are designed to meet.

Table 4. Summary of ACE Activities and the CCSS for ELA/Literacy

ACE Activities	CCSS for ELA/Literacy (All Texts)	CCSS for ELA/Literacy (*The Secret Garden*)
Reading grade-level text	RL.4.10	
Extended and embedded vocabulary instruction	RL.4.4	
Partner talks and other peer work	SL.4.1, L.4.1	
Answering questions using text-based evidence	RL.4.1, SL.4.3	RL.4.2, RL.4.3
Writing to a mainstream lesson prompt	W.4.4, W.4.9, L.4.1, L.4.2	W.4.2
Mini-lessons in vocabulary strategies	L.4.4	
Mini-lessons in language features	L.4.5	L.4.5b
Mini-lessons in background knowledge	RL.4.1, W.4.9	
Language analysis	L.4.1	
Writing summaries	W.4.4, L.4.1, L.4.2	

Reflection Questions and Action Plans

The following reflection questions can be used to prepare to adopt the ACE approach for classroom use. They are adapted from *Key Principles for ELL Instruction* prepared by Understanding Language (January 2013, Stanford University).[11]

Reflect on the kind of reading and writing instruction you are currently providing to support your ELLs. Is this instruction aligned to rigorous, grade-level standards? Does reading instruction help develop conceptual understanding and language competence in tandem? Does writing instruction help ELLs write to sources and produce different genres of writing?

- Action: Support ELLs so that they can access challenging, grade-appropriate curricula.

Reflect on how you make text comprehensible to ELLs. Does instruction provide deliberate and appropriate scaffolds? Does it foster ELL autonomy by equipping students with strategies necessary to comprehend and use language in a variety of settings? ELLs need the types of support described in the ACE approach, because they are acquiring English proficiency and content knowledge concurrently (August & Shanahan, 2006).

- Action: Augment mainstream lessons to provide comprehensive support to ELLs, including learning strategies.

Reflect on the use of students' first languages in your instruction. Do ELLs have an opportunity to draw on their first language knowledge and skills? ELLs come to U.S. classrooms with a tremendous resource at their disposal: their first-language knowledge and skills. Incorporating and building on this resource can aid their comprehension of content delivered in their second language (Dressler & Kamil, 2006).

- Action: Help ELLs acquire strategies such as cognate use that enable them to bootstrap on their first-language knowledge and skills in all instructional contexts.

Reflect on how your classroom is set up, and the types of interactions ELLs have with you and with their peers. What kinds of opportunities do ELLs have for interactions with teachers and peers? ELLs at all levels benefit from regular and ongoing classroom interactions with peers and teachers (Gersten et al., 2007). Interaction with peers may be supported through partner as well as small-group work.

- Action: Strategically pair students so that more proficient students can provide guidance to less proficient students.

Reflect on how you differentiate instruction for ELLs at different proficiency levels. How are the needs of all ELLs being met? It is important to ensure that all students in a classroom receive the support they need.

- Action: Carefully consider the needs of all students in a classroom, differentiate instruction based on student needs, and reduce support as students become more adept.

Reflect on the types of assessment you use. How are diagnostic tools and formative assessment practices employed to measure students' content knowledge, academic language competence, and participation in disciplinary practices? A broad research base, embracing studies of motivation, metacognition,

---

[11] The lead author is a member of the steering committee that drafted these principles.

---

self-regulation, classroom assessment, teachers' discourse practices, and feedback supports the significance of formative assessment in improving student learning (e.g., Bell & Cowie, 2000; Ruiz-Primo & Furtak, 2006; Shepard, 2000).

- Action: Use assessments to guide instruction.

Suggested Activities

The following activities provide an opportunity to practice the ACE approach.

- Select a text that is grade-level appropriate for your mainstream students. Analyze the features in the text that would be challenging for ELLs.

- Using the First 4000 Words list, choose high-frequency vocabulary that you would teach to ELLs. Select four to five of the most abstract words for extended instruction. Identify strategies to embed instruction for the remaining words.

- Choose one or two topics for background knowledge instruction, and select one language feature for a mini-lesson for ELLs.

- Using a mainstream question, create additional supplemental questions for ELLs, along with sentence frames and a word bank.

- Choose one complex sentence, and design a language analysis chart for ELLs.

- Using a mainstream writing prompt, create scaffolds for ELLs, including a graphic organizer and paragraph frame.

Older Emergent Bilinguals' Academic Literacy Development

Sandra Mercuri, University of Texas at Brownsville

Natascha Yarussi, A.P. Solís Middle School, Donna, Texas

This chapter describes the collaboration with a fifth-grade teacher, Ms. Yarussi, in the integration of the language arts curriculum into a science inquiry unit. We begin by describing the context of the school and the demographics of the classroom in which the pedagogical practice was applied and observed. We developed this interdisciplinary unit of inquiry and connected it to the Common Core State Standards for English Language Arts and Literacy in History/Social Studies, Science, and Technical Subjects (CCSS for ELA/Literacy; National Governors Association Center for Best Practices & Council of Chief State School Officers, 2010) and the Next Generation Science Standards (NGSS; National Research Council, 2013) in an attempt to understand how the opportunities for content and language development presented by the standards can be actualized by the emergent bilingual population in Ms. Yarussi's classroom. We borrowed the term *emergent bilinguals* from García, Kleifgen, and Falchi (2008), who explain that "English language learners are in fact *emergent bilinguals*." That is, through school and through acquiring English, these children become bilingual, able to continue to function in their home language as well as in English, their new language and that of school.

Ms. Yarussi works at a Title I school located in an urban area in a southern part of the United States. The school serves 539 first through fifth graders, out of which 489 are economically disadvantaged, 337 are labeled ELLs, and 508 are at risk. The school has a 98% Hispanic population. There is a high rate of delinquency, violence, and gang activity in the area. Among students in the upper grade levels, there is a general resentment toward learning, and most of the students are aware that they consistently perform at the lowest levels, for they refer to themselves as the "ghetto" kids even though they are quite successful in Ms. Yarussi's class.

In this particular classroom, there are 25 students, out of which 22 are labeled ELLs, and 3 are in their second year of monitoring. Twenty-four of these students are Hispanic, and the other is African American. Most of the students are at the intermediate level of language proficiency in reading and writing and at the advanced level in listening and speaking. Only one student is at the beginning level in all language domains.

Ms. Yarussi holds three different certifications: English language arts, English as a second language, and science. She is a native speaker of Spanish and has 16 years of experience teaching within and outside the United States. Ms. Yarussi has the adequate skills to apply the expectations of the CCSS for ELA/Literacy and of articulating reading, writing, listening, and speaking across all content areas. She is a literacy teacher but also a content teacher, and the interdisciplinary curriculum she creates clearly reflects her understanding of the importance of teaching disciplinary literacy and unpacking the linguistic demands of texts and tasks for her emergent bilingual students. In the following sections, we describe how Ms. Yarussi considered content and language demands to design an interdisciplinary unit of inquiry on weather and weather changes to address the linguistic needs of her emergent bilingual students. This teacher prioritized the importance of embedding literacy in the content area of science. Through this integrated approach to teaching science and language arts, the teacher facilitated the development of disciplinary literacy by using multiple types of texts and engaging the students with diverse oral and written tasks around the topic of weather and weather changes.

The CCSS and Specific Demands for Older Emergent Bilinguals

There is growing evidence that schools are not meeting the needs of emergent bilinguals, who are falling behind in both academic language development and content knowledge learning. According to the national assessment's results (Rampey, Dion, & Donahue, 2009), there is a large gap between ELLs and their English-only counterparts on achievement scores in science (72% of fourth graders performed at the basic level or partially mastered the content). In addition, the literacy results for ELLs show that only 4% of fourth-grade ELLs scored at the proficient or advanced levels. A closer look at the new CCSS for ELA/Literacy reveals that the standards present new and complex challenges for students, especially those learning English as a second language. Students are now required to analyze complex texts, use academic vocabulary, and write logical, research-based arguments.

With this in mind, we selected the topic for the unit of inquiry and began the planning stage, taking into consideration the complexity required by the new standards. While we developed a 6-week-long interdisciplinary unit, for the purpose of this chapter, we identified the salient set of standards that aligned with our focus on informational texts throughout the unit, presented here in Table 1.

Following Bunch, Kibler, and Pimentel's (2013) concept of *macro scaffolding* as the integration of language and content within and across lessons and units, and *micro scaffolding* as the integration of strategies to make the input comprehensible in everyday teaching, we developed a series of tasks that required all four language domains based on a series of different informational texts. We discussed not only the content but also how to teach it and how we could embed the language throughout the unit, including support before reading and during the different tasks as well as

Table 1. CCSS for ELA–Literacy and NGSS

CCSS for ELA/Literacy	Standard
College and Career Readiness Anchor Standards for Reading CCRA.R.2	Determine central ideas or themes of a text and analyze their development; summarize the key supporting details and ideas.
Reading Informational Text RI.5.4	Determine the meaning of general academic and domain-specific words and phrases in a text relevant to a *Grade 5 topic or subject area.*
Language L.5.6	Acquire and use accurately grade-appropriate general academic and domain-specific words and phrases, including those that signal contrast, addition, and other logical relationships (e.g., *however, although, nevertheless, similarly, moreover, in addition*).
NGSS—Earth and Space Science Earth Systems 2.D	Climate describes patterns of typical weather conditions over different scales and variations. Historical weather patterns can be analyzed to make predictions about future weather.

a stronger focus on oral responses and collaboration before the students were required to work independently. Our intent was to provide Ms. Yarussi's emergent bilinguals with the tools to meet the standards' challenging academic demands.

In terms of content demands, the students needed to learn science content in reference to weather and weather conditions. Moreover, due to the interdisciplinary nature of the unit, the students also needed to learn the content of language arts defined as the ability to comprehend grade-level texts, acquire and use vocabulary that is relevant to a Grade 5 subject area, and participate in academic discussions and writing tasks on the topic of study in small groups and with the whole class. In addition to the content demands identified, we also identified linguistic demands associated with vocabulary, sentence structure, text density, and discourse patterns. The academic demands of this unit required students to read and write more, to use grammar and vocabulary more accurately, and to master an extensive range of linguistic features (Fang & Schleppegrell, 2008). Scarcella and Merino (2005) explain that teachers should integrate rigorous science concepts with explicit instruction of academic literacy, and they should give equal attention to both. The unit we describe here exemplifies this type of integration.

This integrated approach also allowed us to address the linguistic demands of the unit at three levels: (1) text/discourse level, (2) sentence level, and (3) lexical or word level (Freeman & Freeman, 2009). The text level is often equated with the genre the students must navigate to negotiate meaning in each discipline. The sentence level focuses on the forms or grammatical structures in context. Ms. Yarussi uses sentence stems or frames to support the academic language of her emergent bilinguals. These frames help students create language patterns associated with the content area of science, foster comprehension, and facilitate the acquisition of content-related skills. In addition, it enhances oral participation and increases success in writing assignments (Mercuri &

Rodríguez, 2013). Finally, the word level focuses on three types of vocabulary words: (1) content specific (technical terms particular to the disciplines), (2) general academic (academic terms used across different content areas or multiple-meaning words), and (3) signal words or words that show relationship of ideas (Freeman & Freeman, 2009).

Taking into consideration the linguistic and content demands of the unit, we engaged students in multiple literacy events through inquiry-based learning that involved all four language domains, and we provided multiple scaffolds to facilitate language and content learning throughout the unit of study (Mercuri & Ebe, 2011). In addition, this pedagogical practice motivates students to actively participate in engaging critical thinking exercises around topics that relate to current events such as global warming.

Rationale

Mercuri and Ebe (2011) summarized several national and international organizations' statements regarding instruction that supports the development of content and language for emergent bilinguals. These statements provide research-based findings that can guide teachers as they plan meaningful instruction for emergent bilinguals. Among some of those recommendations is the organization of the curriculum around units of inquiry. Other researchers (Collier & Thomas, 2009; Echevarria & Short, 2010; Gibbons, 2009; Freeman, Freeman, & Mercuri, 2005) have also discussed several reasons for organizing curriculum that has an emphasis on teaching language through content around units of inquiry for emergent bilinguals. First, inquiry-based curriculum moves away from traditional, regimented, teacher-centered instruction. Second, it promotes hands-on experiences that provide a natural teaching ground for building vocabulary and background knowledge for students (Fisher & Frey, 2009; Huerta & Jackson, 2010). In addition, because students revisit concepts across disciplines, English language instruction is more comprehensible (Freeman, Freeman, & Mercuri, 2005).

An enriching inquiry-based curriculum, as shown in this unit, focuses on teaching language through science content. Also, literacy is embedded throughout the unit, providing opportunities for students to transact with different types of text and to use language for real purposes as they engage in academic discussions and write about weather and weather changes using evidence to justify their scientific explanations (Zembal-Saul, McNeill, & Hershberger, 2013; McNeill & Krajcik, 2012). Furthermore, because we integrated one content area such as science with language arts, we promoted authentic reading and writing experiences across the curriculum. While this is an uncommon practice, upper grade and secondary teachers should understand the new reconceptualization of language as *action* that happens across content areas and in all aspects of the students' daily life. They should apply this integrated approach to their teaching given that language and literacy are integral to the pedagogical practices of the content-area classroom. Wong Fillmore and Fillmore (2012) propose that teachers working with emergent bilinguals should deconstruct the text they read and the models of writing they expect their students to be able to access by looking closely at language one sentence at a time. This will help students unpack the information compacted into academic texts and to understand the relation between specific linguistic patterns and the functions they serve in texts in different disciplines as required by the CCSS for ELA/Literacy.

In Ms. Yarussi's classroom, the integration of language, literacy, and content throughout the unit facilitated grade-level language and content development for her students. For example, in this unit the students learned about weather and weather changes. They read fiction and nonfiction books as well as scientific articles about weather and weather changes, sang songs or read poems about the topic to learn and practice new vocabulary, did hands-on projects, and wrote scientific explanations to foster literacy development, including drawings. These types of interrelated activities allow teachers to address language arts and science standards in a meaningful and more authentic way, and they allow students to learn grade-level content, understand the linguistic demands of the discipline, and acquire the academic literacy needed to achieve in schools.

Pedagogical Practice

We began planning our unit using a modified Understanding by Design (UBD; Wiggins & McTighe, 2005) template. First, we identified the CCSS for ELA/Literacy and NGSS standards that we were going to cover throughout the unit. We had extended conversations about what we expected the students to be able to understand, know, and do as they moved through the unit with full participation. In addition, in order to help Ms. Yarussi's emergent bilinguals think critically about weather and weather changes as well as the characteristics of different types of texts, we developed essential questions to guide the teaching and learning of this unit and to engage the students in meaningful meaning-making tasks. Second, we designed different assessments to measure the achievement of the desired results planned for the unit. Third, we planned the lessons and learning activities keeping in mind the goals and essential questions of the unit. Each learning task reflects a clear understanding of the students' abilities, the standards to address, and the scaffolding needed to make every lesson a successful learning event for all students in the class. Figure 1 summarizes the unit of study using an adapted UBD template.

This 6-week interdisciplinary unit of inquiry was divided by different contents and text genres. The focus of the first 2 weeks was on informational texts. Weeks 3 and 4 emphasized narrative texts, and the last 2 weeks of the unit addressed opinion texts. For the purpose of this chapter, we will only discuss salient activities suggested for the first 2 weeks of the unit that focus on informational texts.

Ms. Yarussi introduced the unit to the students through a gallery walk activity. Students were exposed to various pictures spread around the classroom depicting different forms of extreme weather conditions and possible outcomes. Students were asked to walk around and to post questions, impressions, and comments as a way to foster prior knowledge, build schema, and arouse their curiosity. The teacher provided sentence stems for students who needed assistance to actively participate in the activity. Some of the sentence stems provided were:

This is _____.

This reminds me of _____.

I would like to know _____ _____.

Is it true that _____?

I did not know that _____.

Unit Background

Unit Title: Weather and Weather Changes **Grade Level:** 5th grade
Subject Area: ELA/ESL–Science   **Time Frame:** Six Weeks

Brief Summary: In this unit, students will develop their linguistic abilities in English, incorporating into their schema important scientific vocabulary in combination with the understanding and use of literary elements, such as summarization, main idea, theme, inferencing, comparing and contrasting, distinguishing fact from opinion, and recognizing causes and effects. Students will be exposed to different genres of writing, and will compose various papers and projects that will help foster a better understanding of the unit. Students will additionally understand the importance of the weather and weather changes, through the thorough study of informational texts found in varied sources, and the supplement of the science fiction movie, *The Day After Tomorrow* (Emmerich, 2004)

Desired Results

Goal
The unit's goal will be to develop our ability to discuss, read about, write about, and understand the importance of weather and weather changes using the English language.

Standards

Understandings
Students will understand . . .
- How to use the English language to discuss, read about, write about, and understand oral presentations on weather and weather changes.
- Weather types and changes.
- How to research for information.
- How to make connections with informational texts and other forms of literature.
- How to distinguish facts from fiction.
- How to categorize and highlight the importance of our weather and its changes.

Essential Questions
- Why do we use English to carry out academic discussions?
- What are the most important characteristics of informational texts, and how can we use those to enhance connections to other sorts of texts?
- What are the most important characteristics of narrative and opinion texts, and how can we use those to enhance connections to other sorts of texts?
- Where and how do weather conditions happen?
- What are the causes and effects of the different types of weather?
- What is important to know about weather changes and extreme weather conditions?
- How important is it to understand the causes and consequences of global warming?

Knowledge
Students will know . . .
- Content academic vocabulary.
- How to make logical connections within and between texts.
- Main idea and supporting details.
- Summarization of informational and fictional pieces.
- A variety of complete sentences.
- The use of conventions of punctuation and capitalization.
- How to write an informational/narrative/opinion text.
- How to construct argument from evidence.

Skills
Students will be able to . . .
- Analyze the development in informational/narrative and opinion texts.
- Synthesize and make logical connections between and across texts.
- Evaluate main ideas and supporting details.
- Summarize important ideas.
- Identify and write complete sentences.
- Apply proper punctuation and capitalization.
- Write informational pieces.
- Write arguments based on evidence.
- Do critical thinking in relation to evidence provided.

(Continued on page 119)

Performance Task

After a thorough analysis of the weather and weather changes, students will be required to categorize and differentiate the different causes and effects of weather and weather changes, analyze and discuss factual information on recent discoveries, and conduct research on different extreme weather conditions. Students will be required to do critical thinking, and compare and contrast varied sources of information. Students will write informational, narrative, and opinion pieces in different forms and will construct arguments based on evidence. Students will recognize and use the different stages of the writing process and conduct oral presentations.

Criteria

Understanding
- Show a deep and significant understanding of the weather and weather changes.

Reasoning
- Make significant connections with the different sources of information.

Accuracy
- Consistently use ideas and facts used throughout the different readings and discussions held in class.
- Properly use punctuation and capitalization conventions.

Communication
- Elaborate ideas in a sequential and descriptive manner.

Other Evidence
- Oral or written response to the different Essential Questions previously stated.
- Oral and written response to the different topics for research.
- Daily class discussion.

Figure 1. Modified Understanding by Design Template—Weather and Weather Changes

Following the gallery walk, the students watched a video on the different atmospheric layers, and, as they did, they represented the layers using a quarter of a paper plate, coloring and labeling each one of the layers (Figure 2). Students transacted with the information provided as they recalled some of the main characteristics for each layer through a guided whole-class discussion. The linguistic and content demands of the information they accessed through the video was supported by the teacher's "chunking" of the video and prompting questions as they completed the atmospheric layers' project.

To apply this new knowledge and to facilitate the academic discourse of the discipline, Ms. Yarussi engaged her emergent bilinguals in a language experience approach activity to write an informational text on the different atmospheric layers, paying close attention to the formatting of the text and highlighting transitional words such as *in contrast with, especially, in addition to*, and so forth.

Following the writing activity and in groups, the students read two articles from the magazine *Time for Kids* (Plasket, 2012) and from *Mail Online* (Leonard & Reily, 2012) describing the story of Felix Baumgartner's free-fall jump through the different atmospheric layers. As they transacted with the texts, the students applied this new knowledge as they built a two-fold graphic organizer identifying the atmospheric layers and Baumgartner's experience as he went through them.

The groups shared their organizers and explained their findings to the rest of the class using academic language of the unit such as *troposphere, stratosphere, mesosphere, thermosphere*, and *exosphere*, and used sentence frames as needed. Some of the structures provided by the teacher were:

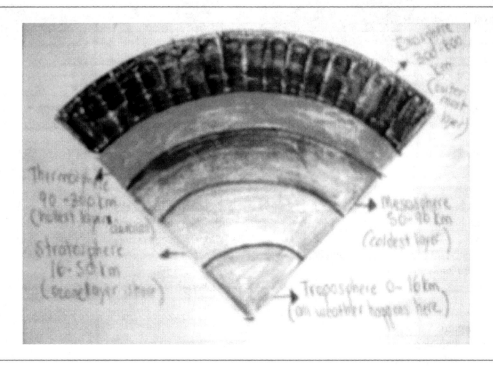

Figure 2. Layers of the Atmosphere

We found out that_____. The experience lasted_____.
First, the_____. Second, the_____.
In addition, _____. We conclude that_____ because
_____.

In order to transition to the next topic and to help students make conceptual connections across readings and among the scientific ideas presented, Ms. Yarussi explained that the main weather changes that we experience happen in the troposphere.

After chorally reading a text on thunderstorms, students completed a graphic organizer with the main points about thunderstorms: characteristics, causes, possible outcomes, and how to be prepared for them. Then, in small groups, students were assigned to a weather condition, and as they transacted with the assigned text, they completed a similar graphic organizer like the one they had completed as a whole class with the teacher's guidance. In turns, students presented the information gathered to the rest of the class, and each student added their classmates' information to their own graphic organizer. After the group presentation, Ms. Yarussi asked the students to identify and define the new vocabulary related to weather and weather changes. These new vocabulary words were studied and analyzed using vocabulary cards and were later included in the unit's science word wall. The vocabulary card included some of the following categories: (a) definition, (b) synonym, (c) antonym, (d) part of speech, (e) the word in a sentence, (f) cognate, and (g) picture. In addition, students completed a Venn diagram with a partner (using paper plates) comparing and contrasting weather conditions and using the new terms. Once the graphic organizers were completed, the teacher provided a model (Figure 3) of a comparison–contrast paragraph, highlighting important characteristics of the text, such as the use of transitional words, connectors,

There are many _____. One weather condition is

_____. Another weather condition is_____.

_____ and _____ are similar in that _____

_____. On the contrary, _____ and _____ are

different in that _____ but _____.

I conclude that _____ because _____

_____.

Figure 3. Paragraph Writing Model for Compare and Contrast

punctuation, and main and secondary ideas. Using this model and the information they gathered in the graphic organizer, the students wrote their own comparison–contrast paragraphs following the model presented by the teacher.

To provide further practice with content and academic language of the unit, Ms. Yarussi organized the students in an inner-outer circle activity. The students exchanged their papers for editing and looked for the use of indentation, capitalizations, punctuation, spelling, and content-specific vocabulary they learned.

Inquiry-based learning includes hands-on activities, explorations, and reasoning (Zembal-Saul, McNeill, & Hershberger, 2013). With this in mind, we selected parts of the movie *The Day After Tomorrow* (Emmerich, 2004) to contextualize the concept of extreme weather conditions and developed a series of labs on weather changes. The students watched the video and summarized it using the structure *who, wanted, but, so, then* to help them identify and analyze the parts of a narrative. They also discussed with the teacher the guiding question: What are the causes and effects of weather changes? They explained their points of view based on experiences they had with extreme weather. The following is an example of one student's summary of the movie:

> Jack, a scientist specialized in climate [*who*], wanted [*wanted*] to warn the public about a possible global climate change as a consequence of global warming. However [*but*], before he was able to do it, a series of sudden climate changes alerted the world. *So* [*so*], after thousands of people died, the public finally [*then*] understood the devastating effects of global warming.

In addition, Ms. Yarussi explained the use of evidence to support their findings as they constructed arguments about the different labs on weather changes. She provided the students with an evidence-based writing scaffold (McNeill & Krajcik, 2012). During a language experience approach activity, Ms. Yarussi completed the evidence-based structure by writing students' responses for each one of the parts of the writing scaffold using the movie as an example (Figure 4).

Students were asked to use this writing scaffold to justify their claims during future experimental activities. Once students understood the concept of weather changes, Ms. Yarussi introduced the labs. She explained the procedures and guided them thoroughly through the steps. She modeled how to record the information for a lab following a lab report format containing the scientific

Claim—The weather is changing. [_____ is _____ or _____ produces
_____.]

Evidence—We have had unusual weather conditions throughout the United States this year. [The evidence to
support my claim is _____.]

Reasoning—Having unusual weather conditions one year does not constitute sufficient evidence to affirm that
the weather is changing. [I agree with _____in that _____.]

Rebuttal—No, [I disagree with _____ in that _____] but because we have had extreme
weather changes, the glaciers are melting and scientists have been observing these patterns for a long time,
we can say that the weather is changing. [Thus, _____ causes _____.]

Figure 4. Weather Changes Writing Scaffold

Source: McNeill and Krajik (2012)

method steps and general academic terms: *observation, hypothesis, materials, procedures, results,* and *conclusion.* Students were asked to pay close attention to the signal words used when writing the procedures that show sequence: *first, second, third, fourth, last.* In small groups, students worked on the signal words as they completed lab reports, following the example provided by the teacher, and discussed and wrote their claims by using the language structures provided. Some of the weather and weather changes labs required were Clouds in a Bottle, Tornado in a Jar, Lightning in Your Mouth, and Make Thunder.

This type of activity fosters academic discussion and scientific writing. It allows the students to enter the community of science as experts as they discuss, learn, and do science in school. To conclude this first part of the unit, students played a teacher-made "jeopardy" game as a way to review key information on weather and weather changes and content-area vocabulary. The jeopardy game had several categories such as weather changes, severe weather, and types of weather. The following is an example of one of the categories:

Storms that have the most powerful winds (reaching 300 mph) ➔ Tornado

Summary and Concluding Thoughts

The pedagogical practice we describe allowed us to thoroughly address the selected CCSS for ELA/Literacy and NGSS standards through different strategies that made the content and linguistic demands of the unit accessible to all students. We were able to accomplish that due to the spiraling nature of the unit we developed. Through the unit, all four language domains were targeted. Multiple opportunities for academic discussion about the topic of study were provided for students. Most of the activities included the reading of a text by the teacher or by the students in groups. In addition, different types of graphic organizers were used to dissect the linguistic complexity of the texts and to gather and organize information. Furthermore, linguistic support was always provided for the students at the beginning stages of language proficiency, which enabled them to understand the ways of participating in the classroom community, in this case a scientific community, as they learned and did science (Prain & Hand, 2006) with the teacher through the different unit activities. Table 2 presents a summary of the linguistic demands of the unit and the support provided for the students by the teacher.

The uncommon practice of embedded literacy in the content areas in most upper elementary and secondary classrooms comes to life in Ms. Yarussi's classroom as she teaches read-write-and-do science with her students throughout the unit activities described in this chapter. Students were

Table 2. Academic Language Demands of the Unit and Support Provided by Teacher

Activity	Discourse Level	Sentence Level	Lexical Level
Video and readings	Definition	I learned that _____ ____. The atmosphere has _____. The layers of the atmosphere are ____, ___, ____, and _____. In the stratosphere we find _____ _____. A characteristic of _____ is ____ ____.	atmosphere troposphere stratosphere mesosphere thermosphere ionosphere exosphere
Graphic organizer (T-chart) for readings and Language experience approach	Summary	In the article titled _____ by _____ we found out that _____. First, _____. Second, _____. In addition, _____. We conclude that _____.	atmosphere in addition troposphere first stratosphere second mesosphere last thermosphere ionosphere exosphere
Venn diagram graphic organizer and Compare–contrast paragraph writing	Comparison	There are many _____. One weather condition is _____. Another weather condition is_____. _____ and _____ are similar in that _____. On the contrary, _____ and _____ are different in that _____ but _____. I conclude that _____ because _____.	weather hail weather conditions wind thunderstorms flood tornado hurricane precipitation fog weather map snow air masses while
Video *The Day After Tomorrow* and Writing scaffold for scientific explanation	Explanation	_____ is _____ or _____ produces _____ because _____. The evidence to support my claim is _____. I agree with _____ in that _____. I disagree with _____ in that _____ but _____. Thus, _____ causes _____.	observation hypothesis materials results procedure conclusion first second third last evidence claim reasoning rebuttal

exposed to different genres of writing and did various projects that helped them foster a better understanding of the unit. Students understood the importance of weather and weather changes, through the thorough study of informational texts from varied sources and a clear focus on vocabulary development.

We want to encourage teachers to embrace this new interdisciplinary approach proposed by the CCSS for ELA/Literacy and focusing on the four language domains by (Bunch, Kibler, & Pimentel, 2013)

- reading complex texts to build background knowledge across different content areas of study;

- writing across the curriculum to inform, argue, and analyze using evidence from different sources; and

- participating in group-work, listening to others' perspectives, and presenting ideas orally in order to participate in different communicative events.

Through the planning and implementation of this unit, we can conclude that an interdisciplinary unit of inquiry serves as an effective macro scaffold for the challenging task of teaching content and language to emergent bilinguals. This integrated approach allows teachers at all grade levels to address the challenges presented by the CCSS for ELA/Literacy and NGSS and affords both teachers and students the opportunity to access challenging grade-level curriculum, and to effectively address the language demands of the materials and activities of each unit of study.

Reflection Questions and Action Plans

1. What are some important considerations teachers should have when developing an interdisciplinary unit of inquiry?

2. Complete an *Understanding by Design* template following the sample provided and plan a unit of inquiry for your grade level. What are the most important things to consider before you start the planning process?

3. How would you integrate vocabulary-building activities that are meaningful and authentic to your designed unit? Why is this important?

4. Explain some activities you could design for your unit that show ways teachers can help students achieve the linguistic and content demands of the CCSS for ELA/Literacy and NGSS.

5. Create a chart for differentiated instruction using a domain of your choice and the different proficiency-level descriptors that align with your interdisciplinary unit.

6. Select a CCSS and NGSS standard and identify how you could modify the pedagogical practice or suggested activities we presented in this chapter to fit the standard selected and the needs of the students in your classroom.

Science and Language Arts (Interdisciplinary Unit)						
Domain	Topic	Level 1	Level 2	Level 3	Level 4	Level 5
Writing	Atmospheric Layers (Informational text)	**Produce** words or phrases on atmospheric layers in close connection to graphic organizer in a cloze activity.	**Paraphrase** important information on atmospheric layers with the aid of a cloze activity.	**Separate** different parts of information on atmospheric layers in sections with the aid of a cloze activity.	**Explain** the importance of atmospheric layers, provide examples, and add details to the information in a cloze activity.	**Evaluate** the importance of atmospheric layers and their classification through the use of additional information in cloze activity.

Figure 5. Differentiated Instruction Based on Students' Language Proficiency—Domain: Writing

Suggested Activities

The following are suggested activities that teachers can use to contextualize instruction for students with varied linguistic and academic proficiency levels (see Figure 5). This will enable educators to address both the content and linguistic demands of the subject matter.

1. Use a range of reading materials to expose the students to different genres and texts with different complexity levels. Include multiple opportunities for students' writing across the curriculum. [RI.5.4]

2. Use problem solving and inquiry to integrate explicit instruction with exploratory learning. [NGSS]

3. Plan interdisciplinary units of inquiry to contextualize learning. [NGSS]

4. Use cooperative work to support language and content development and to develop positive interdependence, individual accountability, equal participation, and simultaneous interaction.

5. Ensure that tasks are structured and that linguistic and nonlinguistic (visuals, realia, manipulatives, and graphic organizers) support is provided so that all students have the possibility to be successful. [L.5.6]

6. Teach vocabulary in the context of authentic readings, and purposeful activities and investigations, not in isolation. [L.5.6]

Beyond History: Glimpses Into the Past Through Picture Books

Judith B. O'Loughlin, Language Matters Education Consultants, LLC

The CCSS and Specific Demands for ELLs

One of the key demands of the Common Core State Standards for English Language Arts and Literacy in History/Social Studies, Science, and Technical Subjects (CCSS for ELA/Literacy; National Governors Association Center for Best Practices [NGA] & Council of Chief State School Officers [CCSSO], 2010a) is that all students are required to demonstrate their ability to understand increasingly complex informational readings, crucial for college, career, and workplace readiness. In the *ELA Standards for Reading for Informational Text* at Grade 5, the content demand may ask students to explain procedures, ideas, or concepts found, for example, in historical or scientific text. Students are required to locate specific information and indicate what happened and why (RI.4.3) and explain connections between events, individuals, ideas, or concepts (RI.5.3). The linguistic demand of the standard, linked to text comprehension, requires students to use both sequence words (e.g., *first, second, then, next, after, in the end*) to describe events and conjunctive adverbs (e.g., *finally, also, however, meanwhile, therefore, otherwise*) or adverbial phrases (e.g., *as quickly as, only occasionally, almost as much as, to put it differently*) and transition words (e.g., *before, after, soon, meanwhile*) and phrases (e.g., *in the first place, at the same time, in conclusion*) to explain the "when and why" of the text. Students must be able to demonstrate their understanding through language by which they respond to the text, describing the consequences and end results, as well as use compare and contrast language.

Connected to key ideas and details, the *ELA Standards for Reading for Informational Text* also require students to integrate information from two or more texts (RI.5.9) on the same topic. The content demand of this standard asks students to demonstrate orally and in writing comprehensive subject knowledge focused on the commonalities or differences of information in multiple texts. The linguistic demand, derived from the content demand, asks students to demonstrate their understanding of content through the use of the transition words that consolidate, summarize, restate, compare/contrast, or show consequences of text information.

Finally, the CCSS for *ELA/Literacy Anchor Standard 7 College and Career Readiness* in Reading, for information presented through diverse media, asks students to integrate and evaluate content presented visually, such as illustrations, photographs, drawings, timelines, and so forth, found in conjunction with text of picture books. The content demand of this standard requires students to make connections with content concepts, theme, main idea, and details, as well as academic language that is presented in text and visual media, including illustrations, photographs, charts, tables, as well as online visual resources. The content demand, connected to the linguistic demand, asks learners to metacognitively interpret meaning in visual representations and text, then use academic language to describe such aspects as setting, viewpoint, time order of events, and historical figures, or historical-fiction figures explicating historical events.

In the CCSS for ELA/Literacy approach to measuring text complexity, the three-part triangular model (NGA & CCSSO, 2010b) assists teachers in determining how easy or difficult a particular text will be to read at a particular grade level. The qualitative dimension considers the reader in terms of text purpose, language conventions, and knowledge demands. The quantitative dimension considers such aspects of text as word and sentence length. Reader-and-task considerations, the final dimension, consider whether the text is appropriate for the student, based on the purpose and complexity of the task as well as the reader's knowledge and experience. For ELLs, all three components of the CCSS for ELA/Literacy model of text complexity take on another dimension— the student's second language abilities and background experiences in a nonnative environment. If ELLs are to read and comprehend informational text "independently and proficiently" on grade level and successfully meet the CCSS for ELA/Literacy, they will need support and supplemental resources. The International Reading Association (2012) recognizes the need for support, noting that diverse learners, including ELLs, to succeed at meeting the CCSS for ELA/Literacy, will require varying resources and adjustments in order to make inferences, analyze text structure, and evaluate text evidence.

Why Use Picture Books?

Although picture books have consistently been used within the primary grades for reading instruction, they have not been widely used for content instruction for preadolescent learners in Grades 4–5 and beyond (Martinez, Harmon, & Roser, 2009). Hellman (2003) indicates that any picture book can be interpreted on many different levels and may be used with and appeal to students in middle grades. Lynch-Brown and Tomlinson (2006) note the appeal of more recently published picture books suited for upper elementary and adolescent learners because they are "sophisticated, abstract, or present complex themes, stories, and illustrations . . . [that] are suitable for children 10 and older" (p. 83). For example, topics in picture books now include fiction and nonfiction narratives related to academic-content topics such as war, racism, homelessness, riots, immigration, historical legislation, and so forth. Additionally, picture book illustrations are able to facilitate students' understanding of text (Hibbing & Rankin-Errickson, May, 2003), reduce the "language load" often present in textbooks (Wood & Tinajero, 2002), as well as facilitate language acquisition and academic language learning for ELLs (Miller & Endo, 2004). Miller (1998) reported that historical topics in content texts "tend to be removed from students' familiar experiences and perspectives." Miller further stated that middle-grade students have difficulty making text and personal connections to historical topics and events presented in textbooks. McCann (2007) noted that many students experience frustration when reading classroom materials due to the presentation of information beyond their comprehension level and are frequently unable to decipher the underlying meaning in their textbooks. Using picture books in content-topic study helps to make the historical period and information "come alive" for these learners.

Connecting the text-to-visuals balance in picture book formats, several authors (Giorgis, 1999; Giorgis & Hartman, 2000; Neal & Moore, 1992; Brame, 2000) have pointed out that contemporary society is moving toward a more visual orientation through the increasingly widespread inclusion of technology in everyday lives and this may account for the appeal of the visual format of picture books for upper elementary and middle school students. Bishop and Hickman (1992) suggest that there are different standards for picture books that are suitable for older learners, both in content and visual composition. In support, Fresch and Harkins (2009) suggest that the illustrations in picture books complement or enhance the written word; thus, the illustrations may "fill in the blanks for the young reader" (p. 5). Furthermore, because the illustrations enrich students' understanding and enable them to think critically and analyze both text and pictures, students are able to comprehend the meaning of the text. Complex concepts can be learned more effectively when visuals are provided along with textual information (McDermott, n.d.). Discussing why to teach visual literacy, Bamford (2003) suggests that gaining proficiency in visual literacy involves perception, conception, and developing both visual and linguistic vocabulary. She suggests that the teaching implications of visual literacy involve the development of students' critical thinking, encouraging them to "investigate images and to analyze and evaluate" (p. 5) what they see in order to respond to the questions teachers pose. She further indicates that to become visually literate, it is important that students are able to comprehend the "subject matter" of visual images, including the syntax, or pictorial structure and organization, as well as the vocabulary of the images presented.

Picture books, with a balance of illustrations and text, can facilitate English learners' comprehension of complex content concepts, represent points of view of an historical concept, introduce content vocabulary, and present the complex syntax of written text through a visual format. Learning how to "read" and interpret visually presented information in picture books will help ELLs to not only comprehend and express content concepts, but also help them meet the CCSS for ELA/Literacy Anchor Standard 7 (CCRA.R.7), "Integrate and evaluate content presented in diverse media and formats, including visually and quantitatively, as well as in words" (NGA & CCSSO, 2010a, p. 10).

Academic Historical Content Learning Enhanced With Picture Books

Teachers of ELLs can create units of instruction that meet the CCSS for ELA/Literacy for a content-topic study or a literary theme to build concept background knowledge, as well as provide comprehensible language and convey meaning through visuals and text by using picture books. Preparation for developing picture book lessons for ELLs requires several steps:

1. Determine the content topic to be addressed.

2. Link the topic's conceptual understandings to the CCSS for ELA/Literacy to be addressed.

3. Identify from both grade-level text(s) and state or national content standards the vocabulary and academic language (see Table 4, Example Vocabulary and Academic Language) and content learning ELLs at different proficiency levels must demonstrate orally and in writing. For example, lesson planning in language arts for literature and informational text should provide ELLs with opportunities to integrate the skills of speaking, listening, reading, and writing by making connections through viewing visuals to make meaning from text.

4. Examine the quality and accuracy of the information in the picture books to be included in instruction, using a checklist for the illustrations (see Table 2) and examining the accuracy of information presented in the narration, including vocabulary and other academic words, such as idioms, idiomatic expressions, and collocations.

So, where does the teacher begin? Planning starts with an examination of both the content standards and the CCSS. The topic of the Civil Rights Movement, for example, fits into the National Curriculum for Social Studies (Herczog, 2010) in two themed areas, "time, continuity, and change" (Theme 2), and "power, authority, and governance" (Theme 6). Teachers need to review the CCSS for ELA/Literacy in the area of informational text as well as the Anchor Standards for Reading related to reading visually presented information. Aligning the instructional unit to the content standards, whether social studies, science, or technical subjects, ensures that the instruction meets district, state, and national standards for instruction and prepares students to address the CCSS for ELA/Literacy and other state content standards (see Table 1).

Planning steps may require research and outreach not only through online resources, educational periodicals, and professional journals, but also through community resources. Determining the English language proficiency levels and previous educational experiences in the native culture and in the United States of the ELLs in the grade will help the teacher make decisions about the most appropriate picture book(s), time period, and theme choices to build conceptual background knowledge of the content topic. Additionally, reviewing the content, both depth and breadth of information presented in the target classroom text and other materials, will help determine appropriate choices for ELLs. What is the depth and breadth of the target text, the textbook coverage of the topic for the Civil Rights Movement? To what resources does the text refer, and does the text provide access through supplemental materials, online links, charts, tables, or photographs? How are the vocabulary and academic language presented in the text? Are there resources for new words

Table 1. Planning Steps for Instructional and Formative Assessment Resources: Including Picture Books in Content Studies

Steps	Resources
National Curriculum Standards for Social Studies: Chapter 2—The Themes of Social Studies (National Council for Social Studies, 2013)	http://www.socialstudies.org http://www.socialstudies.org/system/files/images/documents/7404217.pdf
Common Core State Standards for ELA/Literacy, including Reading Standards, Speaking and Listening, and Anchor Standards	http://www.corestandards.org/ELA-Literacy/RI/5 http://www.corestandards.org/ELA-Literacy/SL/5 http://www.corestandards.org/ELA-Literacy/CCRA/R
Picture books and other nontextbooks	School library and media center; public library; Internet searches, journals (International Reading Association, National Council of Teachers of English, School Library Journal, etc.), Teaching Tolerance www.tolerance.org (picture book and other literature reviews) Common Core State Standards, English Language Arts, Appendix B. http://www.corestandards.org/assets/Appendix_B.pdf
English language development proficiency levels/level descriptors to differentiate practice and application of learning by proficiency level	*TESOL PreK–12 English Language Proficiency Standards* (TESOL, 2006) http://www.tesol.org/docs/books/bk_prek-12elpstandards_framework_318 .pdf?sfvrsn=2 *From Paper to Practice: Using TESOL's ELP Standards in PreK–12 Classrooms* (Gottlieb, Katz, & Ernst-Slavit, 2009) http://www.tesol.org/read-and-publish/bookstore/toc/papertopractice_toc
Formative assessment resources for student response	Graphic Organizers, with word and/or phrase banks Sentence Frames for Student-generated Readers' Theatre scripts Story Boards; story cards; or story frames for Student Review/Retell Timelines, with word and/or phrase banks

and phrases introduced, such as glossed words with synonyms or definitions, or chapter and text glossary? What background do the students need to know about the history of slavery or the term "separate but equal" before the Civil Rights legislation? Finally, what do ELLs need to know to comprehend the target text's coverage of the Civil Rights Movement?

By choosing high-quality, content-accurate picture books, teachers can build background knowledge for ELLs studying the Civil Rights Movement. When choosing picture books, ensure that content is current and correct. Visuals must accurately represent and align with text information. Picture books with a balance of text and illustrations, a match of written and visual information, help ELLs at Level 1 (Starting) or 2 (Emerging) (TESOL International Association, 2006) of English proficiency comprehend concepts. Criteria for illustrations include visual representation/ information from text narrative, historical and historical-fiction figures, setting, academic language, and point of view presented. See Table 2 for examples of criteria to determine if the picture book illustration meets the criteria for content-topic study.

Historical and historical-fiction figures used to explicate historical events should be age/grade/topic appropriate for both English learners and native English speakers and represent either people having experienced or observed the concepts being taught. It is important to ensure that there are no negative stereotypes represented in the text or illustrations (i.e., historical figures, settings, events, or artifacts).

When exploring a theme, such as the Civil Rights Movement, it is important to use picture books that illustrate the theme with the historically accurate representation of genders, races, ethnicities, and age groups. ELLs come to the U.S. classroom with a variety of background knowledge and experiences about U.S. historical topics as well as their own culture's history and most likely will not have the requisite background knowledge of the Civil Rights Movement or an understanding of the history of slavery in the United States. Accuracy of information visually represented is key to building this background knowledge. Vocabulary introduced both in phrases/sentences and visually in illustrations should be accurate and build concept understanding for both the target text and picture book. Reviewing sentences, syntax, and paragraph information may help to determine

Table 2. Criteria for Quality of Picture Book Visuals

Criteria	Questions to Consider Yes/No? How? When? (see text examples in next column)	Text Example The Story of Ruby Bridges (Coles, 1995)
Visual narrative–Text narrative match	Do the pictures represent the events described in the text narrative?	"So Ruby began learning how to read and write in an empty classroom, an empty building." Illustration shows a room filled with desks and chairs and only one occupied, by Ruby Bridges.
Historical and historical-fiction figures to explicate historical events	Do the facial expressions and body language match the information described in the text narrative?	"The crowd seemed ready to kill her." Angry crowd waving fists and carrying signs, surrounds Ruby Bridges.
Setting	Does the visual representation of the setting/location of the events match the narrative?	Inside and outside the school, church, courtroom.
Academic language	Are there examples of academic language visually present?	"calm and confident" Ruby's facial expressions when reading aloud demonstrate these adjectives.
Point of view	Who or what is the focus of the visual(s)? Does the focus of the visual change when the narration changes setting, speaker, or event?	Ruby, her family, the teacher, the crowd, the judge, etc. Yes, each part of the narration, focusing on one event, is accompanied by a visual with the same person/persons' point of view.

Adapted from Bamford (2003).

how the picture book will be introduced and reading text practiced (e.g., teacher modeling, realia and artifacts, practiced chorally by students, pair, small-group, or independent reading).

For Level 1 (Starting) and 2 (Emerging) students, with very dense picture book texts (e.g., multiple paragraphs with compound and complex sentence structures), it may be helpful to paraphrase the text and focus on the illustrations for key vocabulary, concepts, and narration of events. For Level 1 (Starting) and 2 (Emerging) students, a careful choice of picture book focusing on "telling" about the Civil Rights Movement through visual information in illustrations and pictures is key.

Creating and using an organizational chart for the unit of instruction, focused on language features and how each picture book addresses the CCSS for ELA/Literacy, helps to prepare lessons and to differentiate students' oral and written practice by proficiency level.

Table 3 presents an overview of the topic (i.e. slavery and civil rights) and Table 4 presents specific examples of academic language needed to speak and write about the content.

Using Table 3 provides teachers with the resources for the next step, developing differentiated performance expectations by proficiency level for ELLs. Note that the main picture book choice in these two lesson-choice examples, texts one (*My Name is Oney Judge*) and three (*Freedom Summer*) have been paired with companion texts of the same period of time, during slavery (*Dave the Potter: Artist, Poet, Slave*) and during the time period from segregations through desegregation (*White Socks Only* and *The Story of Ruby Bridges*). Meeting RI.5.9 requires ELLs to be able to speak or write about a topic knowledgeably through the integration of information from multiple texts on the same topic. The suggested companion picture books help facilitate oral practice for ELs to this standard because picture books explore the topic and set the foundation to meet the standard.

The first set of paired picture books (the building background "anchor" texts) explores the topic of slavery and sets the foundation for understanding the significance of civil rights from the viewpoint of two different slaves, Oney as a "body servant" (she dresses and grooms Martha Washington) and Dave, a slave in Mississippi who crafted jars and inscribed them with his own poems. In both books, the authors describe the types of work the historical figures performed as slaves. Dave, unlike Oney, was literate, and as indicated in the text, most slaves were not permitted to learn to read and write. Although Dave was never physically freed, Oney was. Laban Carrick Hill (2010), the author of *Dave the Potter: Artist, Poet, Slave*, enables readers to infer that Dave was freed through his artistic creations. Oney, through the author's first-person narrative, describes not only her job but also the times in which she lived through plot, timeline, photographs, drawings, and a map. The reader learns about the potter's craft and artistry through the narrative, pictures, and examples of Dave's poetry. The contrasting information about the historical figures' lives provides ELLs with information to address RI.5.9. Teachers can facilitate students' meeting this standard through the introduction of sentence stems using comparative language, graphic organizers such as t-charts and Venn diagrams, as well as storyboard pictures. Figure 1 provides a model for differentiated performance expectations and includes a description of the language domain and support for ELLs at different English proficiency levels.

In the second example (see Table 3, *White Socks Only, Freedom Summer*, and *The Story of Ruby Bridges*), students explore examples of the lives of African American children through child-focused experiences and event-narratives, both fictional and factual, before and after the Civil Rights Acts

Table 3. Companion Picture Books—Language Features of Sample Biography and Historical Fiction

Paired Picture Books	Vocabulary	Language Features Collocations	Text Features
My Name is Oney Judge Genre: historical fiction; based on the life of a slave Plot: "Body servant" to Martha Washington; freed by George Washington in his will	• servant • enslavement • fugitive • protest • abolitionist	• slave catchers • natural life • enslaved Africans • coded language • saltwater Negro	Metaphor: " I could taste freedom." (Turner, 2010) Text additions: timeline and glossary
Dave the Potter: Artist, Poet, Slave Genre: biography Plot: Slave who could read and write	• withstand • wood ash • repent • artist • poet • slave • carved • epitaph	• plain and basic • like pulling a rabbit out of a hat	Symbolic language: "Dave belongs to Mr. Miles." (Carrick Hill, 2010)
Freedom Summer Genre: historical fiction Plot: Negative effects of desegregated public places	• allowed • asphalt	• step-by-stepping-it • just-washed • quick beat • good-luck nickel	Simile: "His face is like a storm cloud." (Wiles, 2001)
White Socks Only Genre: historical fiction Plot: Segregated drinking fountains before legislation	• prancing • sobbing • bravery • defiance • evoke • brim (hat)	• spit can • snuff juice	Simile: ". . .still as a statue." (Coleman, 1996)
The Story of Ruby Bridges Genre: biography Plot: Enters a formerly all-White school after desegregation order	• federal marshals • irritable • persuade • budge	• long and hard • lunch pail • a long time ago	Symbolic language: "in the middle of an angry mob"; "some people tried to take the law into their own hands." (Coles, 1995) Text additions: biographical afterword

of 1957 and1964. The three picture book examples address RI.5.9 using several texts on the same topic. Although the standard, RL5.9, is the same, the readings focus on a different time period, providing before and after narratives about the Civil Rights Acts of 1957 and 1960.

White Socks Only (Coleman, 1996) unfolds before the Civil Rights Act of 1957 and describes the journey of a young black girl who drinks from a "Whites only" water fountain in Mississippi and relates what happened as a result of her action. *The Story of Ruby Bridges* (Coles, 1995) describes

Table 4. Example Vocabulary and Academic Language for Use With Ramer (2013) Resource

Vocabulary	Collocations	Academic Language/Phrases
burial	more than one dozen	etched in stone
petition/petitioned	deaf ears	public tyranny and slavery are alike detestable to minds conscious of the equal dignity of human nature
inherent	burial ground	posthumous emancipation
injustice	social justice	

the story of the first African American children to integrate into all-White schools in 1960 New Orleans, after the Civil Rights Act of 1957 abolished separate-but-equal public education. Finally, *Freedom Summer* (Wiles, 2001) tells the story of two young boys, one Black and one White, who attempt to go swimming in the local town pool after the Civil Rights Act of 1964 abolished segregation of public places, only to find out that the pool had been filled with cement, thus preventing integration of the facility.

TESOL Standard 5: *English language learners communicate information, ideas, and concepts necessary for academic success in the area of social studies.* (TESOL, 2006)

Common Core State Standard for ELA/Literacy RI.5.9: *Integrate information from several texts on the same topic in order to write or speak about the subject knowledgeably.*

Grade level: 5

Topic: Background information about slavery

Language domain: Speaking

Level 1— Starting	Level 2— Emerging	Level 3— Developing	Level 4— Expanding	Level 5— Bridging
Choose two pictures from each picture book to demonstrate an understanding of the differences in the lives of Oney and Dave. Use a single-word or short-phrase word bank to state the differences.	Using a storyboard graphic organizer, with each frame divided in half, show 2–3 examples of the different lives of two slaves, Dave and Oney. With a partner, using a word bank, orally describe in single words or short phrases, the depicted differences.	Using a t-chart using a sentence stem (e.g., Oney's life was different from Dave's) completed with a partner, orally describe the differences between the lives of two slaves, Oney and Dave.	Using a completed Venn diagram, completed with a partner, orally describe the similarities and differences between the lives of two slaves, Oney and Dave.	Orally describe the differences in the lives of two slaves, through an oral presentation from the first-person viewpoint of one slave, Oney or Dave.

Figure 1. Strand of Sample Performance Indicators for Civil Rights/Slavery Reading

Each book presents sequential information about events through illustration and narration, providing access to information for students of all English language proficiency levels. Teacher support to help them meet RI.5.3, to explain interactions between two or more individuals, events, or ideas in the specific information of the text, is possible with each picture book, as is meeting RI.5.9, through integrating information from multiple texts on the same topic to write or speak knowledgeably.

Lesson planning steps for these three picture books, which connect specifically to the introduction of the target classroom text information on the Civil Rights Acts, can begin with different building background activities. Introducing a timeline of historical legislative civil rights information (see Figure 2) provides a foundation for students to understand the experiences of Joe and John in *Freedom Summer* (Wiles, 2001) and Ruby in *The Story of Ruby Bridges* (Coles, 1995). Using the text's single words and phrases (in a word bank), plus viewing illustrations from *White Socks Only* (Coleman, 1996), *Freedom Summer*, and *The Story of Ruby Bridges*, ELLs can build a timeline of important events, drawing and labeling different dates along the timeline.

Mining the illustrations for sequential historical content information, ELLs can create storyboard frames to draw and label information from picture books. Thus, ELLs through brief oral presentations would address RI.5.3 by showing how and why events and ideas develop and interact over the course of the text reading.

A "read-aloud, think-aloud," using the picture book illustrations and text, helps ELLs sequence events, as well as connect the experiences of historical and historical-fiction figures to their own lives through text-to-self and text-to-world connections. As a starting point for addressing RI.5.9 (i.e., to analyze how two or more texts address similar topics), teachers can help students work toward the integration of information through demonstrating and think-aloud practicing with students to make text connections.

Culminating speaking and writing activities—to make concepts come alive—can include role-play or readers' theatre (e.g., "through the eyes of _____") for one or more of the historical figures or historical-fiction figures from these example picture books. A role-play could be appropriate for ELLs at various English language development levels to chorally present short, practiced dialogues representing the viewpoint of one of the main or supporting historical or historical-fiction

1770 Oney Judge born	1800 George Washington frees his slaves in his will	1801 Dave the potter born	1834–1836 *Dave the Potter* signed/dated pottery	1848 Oney Judge dies	May 3, 1858 Last inscribed pottery/artifacts
1838–1860 Underground Railroad *Henry's Freedom Box*	1861–1865 Civil War *Pink and Say*	1868 14th Amendment	Dec. 1, 1955 Rosa Parks' ride *White Socks Only* *Rosa*	1964 Civil Rights Act *Ruby Bridges* *Freedom Summer*	

Figure 2. Timeline From Slavery to the Civil Rights Act of 1964—Historical Events and Picture Book Examples

Story Character: Sentence Starter	Sentence Ending
Girl: The fountain says	"Whites only."
Girl: I have white socks on	so I can drink from this fountain.
Joe: We are going to	float on our backs in the swimming pool.
John Henry: I want to do	everything you can do.
Ruby: Mrs. Henry helped me learn	how to read and write.
Ruby: I was Mrs. Henry's	only student in her classroom.

Figure 3. Role-Play Word and Phrase Bank Examples
Note: Sentence endings can be aligned with sentence starters or mixed up

figures. The dialogues could be written using sentence frames or sentence starters of information (see Figure 3) and practiced by pairs. Example choices and possible characters for role-play could be the following.

- *White Socks Only* (Coleman, 1996)—the young girl going into town without permission; her mother

- *Freedom Summer* (Wiles, 2001)—Joe, John Henry, or John Henry's brother, Will

- *The Story of Ruby Bridges* (Coles, 1995)—Ruby, Ruby's mother, Ruby's teacher, Mrs. Henry

For readers' theatre presentations, more English-proficient learners could help draft the dialogue, choosing essential information for their own historical figure or historical-fiction figure in cooperative writing groups. ELLs with limited English proficiency could recite dialogue chorally with one or two partners. Role-play and readers' theatre could also be used as one type of formative assessment of students' writing, speaking, and use of academic language.

Reflection Questions and Action Plans

1. How could picture book lessons to introduce content concepts be used in classrooms with multiple groups of students, such as a self-contained classroom of mainstream native English speakers, gifted-and-talented, and ELLs at two to three different English language proficiency levels? How would instruction be differentiated to address meeting the CCSS for ELA/Literacy for each of these groups?

2. Because visual literacy is one of the CCSS for ELA/Literacy Anchor Standards, what other types of visuals, including media, technology, apps, and so forth, could be included in a content-topic study to complement content-based picture book choices?

3. Using the steps listed at the beginning of the section Academic Historical Content Learning Enhanced With Picture Books, how could you apply the process to another content study, such as mathematics, science, or an additional social studies topic? How

would your steps in the process be the same? How would they differ? What additional steps might be necessary to analyze the visuals? What texts would be used?

4. Considering a science, mathematics, or an additional social studies topic, what would be an appropriate building background "anchor" for the topic? Ideally, what would be the subject of the picture books, either single books or paired books, to anchor the topic and build background?

Action Plans

Create a lesson plan using picture book resources for a topic in the content areas of social studies, science, mathematics, or technical topics. The steps below will help you develop and implement your action plan. A lesson may require instruction for more than 1 day, depending on the content concept and the standard addressed.

A. Review the content-area curriculum for grade-age appropriate topic. (*Note:* ELLs in a specific age-appropriate grade will have different levels of language development, background knowledge, and experiences in English.)

B. Review content topic, vocabulary (See Table 4, Example Vocabulary and Academic Language), and concepts to determine the CCSS for ELA/Literacy to be addressed in the lesson. (See *Note* in Step A.)

C. Determine which local, state, or national content standards the lesson will address. Make sure the content standard is grade appropriate.

D. Research the parameters of the topic—what aspects of the topic are introduced in the grade level? What background knowledge do ELLs need to comprehend the concepts? (See *Note* in Step A.)

E. Find picture books that accurately cover the topic both visually and through text content. Use Table 3 to record information in preparation for reading and activities. If appropriate, use Figure 2 to organize the picture books.

F. Determine if the picture book is visually appropriate. Use Table 2 to "read" pictures, illustrations, and other visuals. Record information on Figure 2 to organize picture books in an historical timeline (if topic appropriate) or develop another graphic organizer appropriate for your topic. Develop a model lesson, including speaking or writing sample performance indicators for students at five different proficiency levels. See Figure 1.

G. Teachers will need to determine what academic language and concepts students have learned. What formative assessment would work best for this lesson? Will students complete a graphic organizer, answer in choral response, complete drawings/storyboard, participate in a play, or write (e.g., ticket out—respond to a reflection question about the day's learning on a slip of paper, index card, or graphic organizer)?

H. Teach the lesson.

Additional Activities: Using Civil Rights Topic Picture Books

1. Use wordless picture books: For ELLs at lower levels of proficiency, use wordless picture books with rich illustrations. Provide word and phrase banks, along with some strategic sentence frames, and have students work in pairs to take turns describing what is in the illustrations. A good resource is *Unspoken: A Story From the Underground Railroad* (Cole, 2012).

2. Use poetry: For students at the Developing through Expanding levels (TESOL, 2006) introduce the poem *Dreams* (Hughes, 1932). Have ELLs synthesize information from one or two picture books to demonstrate if and how an historical figure in the picture book reached or did not reach his or her dream.

3. Use news media resources: For ELLs at the Developing through Expanding levels introduce a media article from an online or print news resource (e.g., AP, CNN, or local newspaper) connected to the background of the topic (e.g., Ramer, 2013; Wood, 2013). Table 4 gives example language for use with the Ramer (2013) resource. Use both the audio component and the written article to discuss the impact of granting freedom posthumously. Link the discussion to one or more of the building background anchor picture books.

4. Simulation activity. Develop an activity involving students in a separate-but-equal experience. Introduce illogical classroom procedures and rules, randomly assigning students to different groups. Assigning certain rights to each group, favor one group. Debrief the activity. Help students make connections to picture book historical and fiction-historical figures, as well as to themselves (text-to-self, text-to-text, and text-to-world; Keene & Zimmerman, 1997, 2007).

Selected Picture Books for Civil Rights

Bunting, E. (1960). *The blue and the gray*. New York, NY: Scholastic.

Cole, H. (2012). *Unspoken: A story from the underground railroad*. New York, NY: Scholastic.

Coleman, E. (1996). *White socks only*. Chicago, IL: Albert Whitman & Co.

Coles, R. (1995). *The story of Ruby Bridges*. New York, NY: Scholastic.

Giovanni, N. (2007). *Rosa*. New York, NY: Square Fish Books.

Haskins, J. (2005). *Delivering justice: W. W. Law and the fight for civil rights*. Cambridge, MA: Candlewick Press.

Hill, L. C. (2010). *Dave the potter: Artist, poet, slave*. New York: Little, Brown & Company.

Kittinger, J. S. (2010). *Rosa's bus*. Honesdale, PA: Boyds Mills Press.

Levine, E. (2007). *Henry's freedom box: A true story from the underground railroad*. New York, NY: Scholastic.

Polacco, P. (1994). *Pink and say*. New York, NY: Philomel.

Wiles, D. (2001). *Freedom summer*. New York, NY: Aladdin Paperbacks.

Woodson, J. (2001). *The other side*. New York, NY: G. P. Putnam's Sons.

Conclusion

Pamela Spycher, WestEd

It has been said that language is the "hidden curriculum" of schooling (Christie, 1999). When language remains a mystery to students, their access to a world-class education is limited because language is the medium through which we develop our thinking and the medium through which learning takes place in schools (Halliday, 1993). Fortunately, teachers are in a position to demystify language and empower their English learners (ELs) to understand the language resources that English affords and how these resources are used to make meaning. This language awareness supports students in understanding the language they encounter in texts and tasks and gives them options for making informed choices about using language themselves. When ELs have a robust reservoir of language resources at their disposal, along with the language awareness necessary to understand which resources to use and when, they will find it easier to "shift" from more everyday registers[1] to more academic registers when they are expected to do so in school. The chapters in this volume demonstrate how teachers might support their ELs to develop these understandings about English and abilities using English so that they can be successful in school and beyond.

But first, teachers need to have a clear understanding about the language in texts and tasks that may present challenges to their ELs, and to think carefully about the language resources their students need to "build up" so that they can be intentional in supporting their students in expanding their linguistic reservoirs. This intentional approach to language development requires teachers

---

[1] *Register* refers to the combination of vocabulary, grammatical resources, and discourse structures of language that varies depending on who we are interacting with, what we are trying to accomplish, and the mode of our communication.

to think about language in ways that may be unfamiliar, and this has implications for the way we approach professional learning and collaboration as a community of educators. Teachers' deep understandings of how English works and how to teach these understandings requires engagement with the same types of tasks that we expect to see in classrooms with ELs: analytical readings of professional articles and books; collaborative conversations with colleagues about pedagogy, content, and language; seeing things modeled in order to have an idea about what to aim for; the freedom and encouragement to take risks and make mistakes; and the space to openly reflect on and discuss successes and challenges after implementing new approaches. These shifts in professional learning and teacher collaboration are just as important as the shifts we expect to see in classroom instruction.

Understanding and gaining proficiency with academic English across the disciplines opens up possibilities for ELs to understand the world better and to express their ideas more effectively. Developing the capacities of literate individuals is the ultimate goal for all students, as articulated in the CCSS for ELA/Literacy:

> Students can, without significant scaffolding, comprehend and evaluate complex texts across a range of types and disciplines. . . . Students establish a base of knowledge across a wide range of subject matter by engaging with works of quality and substance. They become proficient in new areas through research and study. They read purposefully and listen attentively to gain both general knowledge and discipline-specific expertise. They refine and share their knowledge through writing and speaking. (NGA & CCSSO, 2010, p. 7)

Teachers who understand how to facilitate learning experiences where their ELs engage deeply with content knowledge, interact meaningfully with their peers and with texts, and also learn about how English works to make meaning are in a better position to help their students fulfill their linguistic and academic potential. They are also likely to enjoy the journey infinitely more because they'll see their EL students learn and thrive daily, which is the ultimate reward of the teaching profession.

References

Achieve. (2012). *Educators Evaluating Quality Instructional Products.* Retrieved from http://www.achieve.org /EQuIP

American Psychological Association. (2009). *College dictionary of psychology.* Washington, DC: Author.

Anderson, T., Jess, D., Williams, A. (2000). *Colonial adventures: Charting a course down the coast, second revised edition.* Madison, WI: DEMCO.

August, D., Artzi, L., Barr, C., & Massoud, L. (2013). *The role of explicit instruction and word type in the acquisition of vocabulary by young Spanish-speaking ELLs.* Manuscript in preparation.

August, D., Barr, C., Artzi, L., & Massoud, L. (2013). *Developing vocabulary through storybook reading: Results of an effective vocabulary intervention for young Spanish-speaking ELLs.* Manuscript in preparation.

August, D., & Hakuta, K. (Eds.). (1997). *Improving schooling for language minority children: A research agenda.* Washington, DC: National Academies Press.

August, D., & Shanahan, T. (Eds.). (2006). *Developing literacy in second-language learners: Report of the National Literacy Panel on Language Minority Children and Youth.* Mahwah, NJ: Lawrence Erlbaum.

August, D., & Shanahan, T. (2010). Effective literacy instruction for English learners. In California Department of Education (Ed.), *Improving education for English learners: Research-based approaches* (pp. 209–250). Sacramento, CA: California Department of Education.

Ausubel, D. P. (1968). *Educational psychology: A cognitive view.* New York, NY: Holt, Rinehart and Winston.

Bamford, A. (2003). *The visual literacy white paper.* Commissioned by Adobe Systems Pty Ltd, Australia. Retrieved from http://wwwimages.adobe.com/www.adobe.com/content/dam/Adobe/en/education/pdfs /visual-literacy-wp.pdf

Beck, I. L., McKeown, M. G., & Kucan, L. (2013). *Bringing words to life: Robust vocabulary instruction* (2nd ed.). New York, NY: Guilford Press.

Bell, B., & Cowie, B. (2000). The characteristics of formative assessment in science education. *Science Education, 85*, 536–553.

Biography Channel. (2013). *Charles Richard Drew.* Retrieved from http://www.biography.com/people/charles-drew-9279094

Bishop, R., & Hickman, J. (1992). Four or fourteen or forty; picture books are for everyone. In S. Benedict & L. Carlisle (Eds.), *Beyond words: Picture books for older readers and writers* (pp. 1–10). Portsmouth, NH: Heinemann.

Boyles, N. (2012). Closing in on close reading. *Educational Leadership, 70*(4), 36–41.

Brame, P. B. (2000). Using picture storybooks to enhance social skills training of special needs students. *Middle School Journal, 32*(1), 41–46.

Bransford, J., Brown, A., & Cocking, R. (2001). *How people learn: Brain, mind, experience, and school.* Washington, DC: National Academies Press.

Brisk, M. E., Hodgson-Drysdale, T., & O'Connor, C. (2011). A study of a collaborative instructional project informed by systemic functional linguistics: Report writing in the elementary grades. *Journal of Education, 191*(1), 1–12.

Brown, P., & Abell, S. (2007). Examining the learning cycle. *Science and Children, 44*(5), 58–59.

Bruner, J. (1960). *The process of education.* Cambridge, MA: Harvard University Press.

Bruner, J. (1966). *Toward a theory of instruction.* Cambridge, MA: Harvard University Press.

Bruner, J. S. (1983). *Child's talk: Learning to use language.* New York, NY: Norton.

Bunch, G., Kibler, A., & Pimentel, S. (2013). Realizing opportunities for English learners in the Common Core English language arts and disciplinary literacy standards. *Understanding language: Language, literacy, and learning in the content areas.* Stanford, CA: Stanford University. Retrieved from http://ell.stanford.edu/sites/default/files/pdf/academic-papers

Burnett, F. H. (1911). *The secret garden.* New York, NY: Frederick A. Stokes.

California Department of Education. (2012). *California English Language Development Standards.* Retrieved from http://www.cde.ca.gov/sp/el/er/eldstandards.asp

Californians Together. (2010). *Reparable Harm: Fulfilling the unkept promise of educational opportunity for California's long term English learners.* Long Beach, CA: Laurie Olsen.

Campione, J. C., & Day, J. D. (1981). Learning to learn: On training students to learn from texts. *Educational Researcher, 10,* 14–21.

Christie, F. (Ed.). (1999). *Pedagogy and the shaping of consciousness: Linguistic and social processes.* London, UK: Cassell Academic.

Christie, F., & Derewianka, B. (2008). *School discourse: Learning to write across the years of schooling.* London, England: Continuum.

Cochran-Smith, M. (2004). *Walking the road: Race, diversity and social justice in teacher education.* New York, NY: Teachers College.

Coleman, J., & Goldston, M. (2011). What do you see? *Science and Children, 49,* 42–47.

Collier, V., & Thomas, W. (2009). *Educating English learners for a transformed world.* Albuquerque, NM: Dual Language Education of New Mexico Fuente Press.

Collins, M. F. (2005). ESL preschoolers' English vocabulary acquisition from storybook reading. *Reading Research Quarterly, 40*(4), 406–408.

de Oliveira, L. C., and Dodds, K. N. (2010). Beyond general strategies for English language learners: Language dissection in science. *Electronic Journal of Literacy through Science, 9,* 1–14. Retrieved fromhttp://ejlts.ucdavis.edu

Derewianka, B. (2011). *A New Grammar Companion for Teachers.* Sydney, NSW: Primary English Teaching Association.

Derewianka, B., & Jones, P. (2012). *Teaching language in context.* Melbourne, Australia: Oxford University Press.

Dickinson, D. K., & Smith, M. W. (1994). Long term effects of preschool teachers' book readings on low income children's vocabulary and story comprehension. *Reading Research Quarterly, 29,* 105–122.

Doherty, R. W., Hilberg, R. S., Pinal, A., & Tharp, R. G. (2003). Five Standards and student achievement. *NABE Journal of Research and Practice, 1*(1), 1–24.

Dressler, C., & Kamil, M. (2006). First and second-language literacy. In D. L. August & T. Shanahan (Eds.), *Developing literacy in a second language: Report of the National Literacy Panel* (pp. 123–139). Mahwah, NJ: Lawrence Erlbaum.

Duke, N. K. (2004). The case for informational text. *Educational Leadership, 61*(6), 40–44.

Dutro, S., & Moran, C. (2003). Rethinking English language instruction: An architectural approach. In G. Garcia (Ed.), *English learners: Reaching the highest level of English literacy* (pp. 227–258). Newark, DE: International Reading Association.

Eberback, C., & Crowley, K. (2009). Everyday to scientific observation: How children learn to observe the biologist's world. *Review of Educational Research, 79,* 39–68.

Echevarria, J., & Short, D. (2010). Programs and practices for effective sheltered content instruction. In California Department of Education (Ed)., *Improving education for English learners: Research-based approaches* (pp. 251–322). Sacramento, CA: California Department of Education Press.

Echevarria, J., Vogt, M. E., & Short, D. J. (2008). *Making content comprehensible for elementary English learners.* Boston, MA: Allyn & Bacon.

Elley, W. B. (1989). Vocabulary acquisition from listening to stories. *Reading Research Quarterly, 24*(2), 174–187.

Elley, W. B., & Mangubai, F. (1983). The impact of reading on second language learning. *Reading Research Quarterly, 19*(1), 53–67.

Emmerich, R. (2004, May). *The day after tomorrow.* USA: Twentieth Century Fox.

Fang, Z., Lamme, L., & Pringle, R. (2010). *Language and literacy in inquiry-based science classrooms, grades 3–8.* Thousand Oaks, CA: Corwin.

Fang, Z., & Schleppegrell, M. J. (2008). *Reading in secondary content areas: A language-based pedagogy.* Ann Arbor, MI: University of Michigan Press.

Fillmore, L. W., & Wong-Fillmore, C. J. (2012). What does text complexity mean for English language learners and language minority students? *Understanding language: Language, literacy, and learning in the content areas.* Stanford, CA: Stanford University. Retrieved from http://ell.stanford.edu/sites/default/files /pdf/academic-papers

Fisher, D. (2013). *Close reading and the CCSS.* Retrieved from http://www.mhecommoncoretoolbox.com/ close-reading-and-the-ccss-part-1.html

Fisher, D., & Frey, N. (2009). *Background knowledge: The missing piece of the comprehension puzzle.* Portsmouth, NH: Heinemann.

Fisher, D., Frey, N., & Lapp, D. (2012). *Text complexity: Raising rigor in reading.* Newark, DE: International Reading Association.

Fitzgerald, J., & Graves, M. F. (2004). *Scaffolding reading experiences for English language learners.* Norwood, MA: Christopher Gordon.

Folsom, J., Hunt, C., Cavicchio, M., Schoenemann, A., & D'Amatao, M. (2007). How do you know that? Guiding early elementary students to develop evidence-based explanations about animals. *Science & Children, 45,* 20–25.

FOSS. (2010). *Pebbles, sand, and silt.* Berkeley, CA: Lawrence Hall of Science.

Freeman, D., & Freeman, Y. (2009). *Academic language for English learners and struggling readers.* Portsmouth, NH: Heinemann.

Freeman, Y., Freeman, D., & Mercuri, S. (2005). *Dual language essentials for teachers and administrators.* Portsmouth, NH: Heinemann.

Fresch, M. J., & Harkins, P. (2009). *The power of picture books: Using content area literature in middle school.* Urbana, IL: National Council of Teachers of English.

Furtak, E. M., Seidel, T., Iverson, H., & Briggs, D. (2012). Experimental and quasi-experimental studies of inquiry-based science teaching: A meta-analysis. *Review of Educational Research, 82,* 300–329.

Garcia, E. G., & Bauer, E. B. (2004). The selection and use of texts with young English language learners. In J. Hoffman & D. Schallert (Eds.), *The texts in primary classrooms* (pp. 157–171). Mahwah, NJ: Lawrence Erlbaum.

García, O., Kleifgen, J., & Falchi, L. (2008). *Equity in the education of emergent bilinguals: The case of English language learners.* Research Review Series Monograph. Campaign for Educational Equity. New York, NY: Teachers College Press.

Garza, R. (2009). Latino and White high school students' perceptions of caring behaviors: Are we culturally responsive to our students. *Urban Education, 44,* 297–321.

Gebhard, M., Willett, J., Jimenez, J., & Piedra, A. (2010). Systemic functional linguistics, teachers' professional development, and ELLs' academic literacy practices. In T. Lucas (Ed.), *Preparing all teachers to teach English language learners* (pp. 91–110). Mahwah, NJ: Lawrence Erlbaum/Taylor & Francis.

Genesee, F., Lindholm-Leary, K., Saunders, W., & Christian, D. (2005). English language learners in U.S. schools: An overview of research findings. *Journal of Education for Students Placed at Risk, 10*(4), 363–385.

Gersten, R., Baker, S. K., Shanahan, T., Linan-Thompson, S., Collins, P., & Scarcella, R. (2007). *Effective literacy and English language instruction for English learners in the elementary grades: A practice guide* (NCEE 2007-4011). Washington, DC: U.S. Department of Education.

Gibbons, P. (2002). *Scaffolding language, scaffolding learning: Teaching second language learners in the mainstream classroom.* Portsmouth, NH: Heinemann.

Gibbons, P. (2008). "It was taught good and I learned a lot": Intellectual practices and ESL learners in the middle years. *Australian Journal of Language and Literacy, 31*(2), 155–173.

Gibbons, P. (2009). *English learners, academic literacy, and thinking: Learning in the challenge zone.* Portsmouth, NH: Heinemann.

Giorgis, C. (1999). The power of reading picture books aloud to secondary students (Electronic Version). *The Clearing House, 73*(1), 51–53.

Giorgis, C., & Hartman, K. J. (2000). Using picture books to support middle school curricula. *Middle School Journal, 31*(4), 34–41.

Girard, V., & Spycher, P. (2007). Deconstructing language for ELs. *Aiming high resource.* Santa Rosa, CA: Sonoma County Office of Education.

Gonzalez, N. E., Moll, L. C., & Amanti, C. (Eds.). (2005). *Funds of knowledge: Theorizing practices in households and classrooms.* Mahwah, NJ: Lawrence Erlbaum.

Gottlieb, M., Katz, A., & Ernst-Slavit, G. (2009). *From paper to practice: Using the TESOL ELP standards in preK–12 classrooms.* Alexandria, VA: TESOL International Association.

Grabe, W., & Stoller, F. L. (2002). *Teaching and researching reading.* Harlow, England: Pearson Education.

Graves, M. F., August, D., & Mancilla-Martinez, J. (2012). *Teaching vocabulary to English learners.* New York, NY: Teachers College Press.

Halliday, M. A. K. (1993). Towards a language-based theory of learning. *Linguistics and Education, 5,* 93–116.

Halliday, M. A. K., & Hasan, R. (1989). *Language, context, and text: Aspects of language in a social-semiotic perspective* (2nd ed). Oxford, England: Oxford University Press.

Halliday, M. A. K., & Martin, J. R. (1993). *Writing science: Literacy and discursive power.* London: Falmer.

Hammond, J. (2006). High challenge, high support: Integrating language and content instruction for diverse learners in an English literature classroom. *Journal of English for Academic Purposes, 5,* 269–283.

Hattie, J., & Timperley, H. (2007). The power of feedback. *Review of Educational Research, 77,* 81–112.

Hellman, P. (2003). The role of postmodern picture books in art education. *Art Education, 56*(6), 6–12.

Herczog, M. M. (2010, September). Using the NCSS national curriculum standards for social studies: A framework for teaching, learning, and assessment to meet social studies standards. *Social Education, 74*(4), 217–222. Retrieved from http://www.socialstudies.org/system/files/images/documents/7404217.pdf

Hibbing, A. N., & Rankin-Erickson, J. L. (May, 2003). A picture is worth a thousand words: Using visual images to improve comprehension for middle school struggling readers. *The Reading Teacher, 56*:8, 758–770.

Horowitz, R. (Ed.). (2007). *Talking texts: How speech and writing interact in school learning awareness.* Mahwah, NJ: Lawrence Erlbaum.

Huerta, M., & Jackson, J. (2010). Connecting literacy and science to increase achievement for English language learners. *Early Childhood Education Journal, 38*(3), 205–211.

Hughes, L. (1932). *Dreams.* Retrieved from http://www.poets.org/viewmedia.php/prmMID/16075

International Reading Association. (2012). *Literacy implementation guidance for the ELA Common Core State Standards* [White Paper]. Retrieved from http://www.reading.org/general/AboutIRA/white-papers/ela-common-core-standards.aspx

Justice, L. M., Meier, J., & Walpole, S. (2005). Learning new words from storybooks: An efficacy study with at-risk kindergartners. *Language, Speech, and Hearing Services in Schools, 36,* 17–32.

Keene, E.O., & Zimmerman, S. (1997). *Mosaic of thought.* Portsmouth, NH: Heinemann.

Keene, E. O., & Zimmerman, S. (2007). *Mosaic of thought, second edition: The power of comprehension strategy.* Portsmouth, NH: Heine

Klingner, J. K., Vaughn, S., & Schumm, J. S. (1998). Collaborative strategic reading during social studies in heterogeneous fourth grade classrooms. *The Elementary School Journal, 99*(1), 3–20.

Koehler, H., Martz, T., Montgomery, N., & Kincaid, L. (2010). *The heart circulates blood.* Retrieved from http://www.lakesc.lake.k12.ca.us/lessons/pdf/Grade5_Heart-Circulates-Blood_TLC2010.pdf

Knapp, P., & Watkins, M. (2005). *Genre, text, grammar: Technologies for teaching and assessing writing.* Sydney, Australia: University of New South Wales Press.

Koskinen, P. S., Blum, I. H., Bisson, S. A., Phillips, S. M., Creamer, T. S., & Baker, T. K. (2000). Book access, shared reading, and audio models: The effects of supporting the literacy learning of linguistically diverse students in school and at home. *Journal of Educational Psychology, 92*(1), 23–36.

Lawson, A. E. (1995). *Science teaching and the development of thinking.* Belmont, CA: Wadsworth.

Lee, O. (2002). Science inquiry for elementary students from diverse backgrounds. In W. G. Secada (Ed.), *Review of research in education* (vol. 26, pp. 23–69). Washington, DC: American Educational Research Association.

Lee, O., & Fradd, S. (1996). Literary skills in science learning among linguistically diverse students. *Science Education, 80*(6), 651–671.

Lee, O., Quinn, H., & Valdes, G. (2013). Science and language for English language learners in relation to next generation science standards and with implications for CCSS for English language arts and mathematics. *Educational Researcher, 42,* 223–233.

Lems, K., Miller, L. D., & Soro, T. M. (2010). *Teaching reading to English language learners: Insights from linguistics.* New York, NY: Guilford Press.

Leonard, T., & Reilly, J. (2012, October). *Felix-Baumgartner-headcam-video.* Retrieved from http://www.dailymail.co.uk/sciencetech/article-2217915/Felix-Baumgartner-headcam-video-It-like-Hell-terrifying.html

Levine, L. N., Lukens, L., & Smallwood, B. A. (2013). *The GO TO strategies: Scaffolding options for teachers of English language learners, K–12.* For Project EXCELL, a partnership between the University of Missouri–

Kansas City and North Kansas City Schools, funded by the U.S. Department of Education, PR Number T195N070316. Retrieved from http://webdev.cal.org/development/projects/go-to-strategies.html

Levine, L. N., & McCloskey, M. L. (2013). *Teaching English language and content in mainstream classes: One class, many paths* (2nd ed.). Boston, MA: Pearson.

Lynch-Brown, C., & Tomlinson, C. M. (2006). *Essentials of children's literature, 5th edition*. Boston, MA: Allyn & Bacon.

Mackey, A., & Goo, J. (2007). Interaction research in SLA: A meta-analysis and research synthesis. In A. Mackey (Ed.), *Conversational interaction in second language acquisition* (pp. 407–552). Oxford, England: Oxford University Press.

Mancilla-Martinez, J., & Lesaux, N. K. (2010). Predictors of reading comprehension for struggling readers: The case of Spanish-speaking language minority learners. *Journal of Educational Psychology, 102*(3), 701–711.

Martinez, M., Harmon, J., & Roser, N. (2009). Using picture books with older learners. In K. Wood & W. Blanton (Eds.), *Literacy instruction for adolescents: Research-based practice,* (pp. 287–305). New York, NY: Guilford Press.

Marulis, L. M., & Neuman, S. B. (2010). The effects of vocabulary intervention on young children's word learning. *Review of Educational Research, 80*, 300–335.

McCann, G. T. (2007, December). Reading instruction: A new age for picture books. *NJEA Review, 81*(4), 4–5. Retrieved from http://www.njea.org/pdfs/Review_Dec2007.pdf?1370990029643

McDermott, K. (n.d.). Visual literacy and the use of images in the secondary language arts classroom. Unpublished manuscript. St. Mary's College of Maryland. Retrieved from http://www.smcm.edu/educationstudies/pdf/rising-tide/volume-4/Kathleen-McDermott-MRP1.pdf

McGee, L. M., & Schickedanz, J. A. (2007). Repeated interactive read-alouds in preschool and kindergarten. *The Reading Teacher, 60*(8), 742–751.

McGough, J., & Nyberg, L. (2013). Making connections through conversation. *Science & Children, 50*, 42–46.

McNeill, K., & Krajcik, J. (2012). *Supporting grade 5–8 students in constructing explanations in science: The claim, evidence, and reasoning framework for talk and writing.* Upper Saddle River, NJ: Pearson Education.

Mercuri, S., & Ebe, A. (2011). Developing academic language and content for emergent bilinguals through a science inquiry unit. *Journal of Multilingual Education Research, 2*(spring), 81–102.

Mercuri, S., & Rodríguez, A. (In press). Teaching academic language through an ecosystem unit. In M. Gottlieb & G. Ernst-Slavit (Eds.), *Academic language demands for language learners: From text to context.* Thousand Oaks, CA: Corwin Press.

Merino, B. J., & Ambrose, R. C. (2009). Beginning teacher inquiry in linguistically diverse classrooms. In C. Craig & L. Deretchin (Eds.), *Teacher learning in small-group settings. Teacher Education Yearbook, XVII* (pp. 242–260). Lanham, MD: Rowman & Littlefield.

Merino, B. J., & Dixon, K. (2010). Learning about teaching ELLs through case studies of the inquiry of exemplary new teachers. In C. Faltis & G. Valdez (Eds.), *Education, immigrant students, refugee students, and English learners* (pp. 414–437). New York, NY: Columbia.

Miller, P. C., & Endo, H. (2004). Understanding and meeting the needs of ESL students. *Phi Delta Kappa, 85*, 786–791.

Miller, T. (1998). The place of picture books in middle-level classrooms. *Journal of Adolescent & Adult Literacy, 41*, 376–381.

Minicucci, C. (1996). *Learning science and English: How school reform advances scientific learning for limited English proficient middle school students* (Educational Practice Report No. 17). Santa Cruz, CA: National Center for Research on Cultural Diversity and Second Language Learning.

Nagy, W. E., Garcia, G. E., Durgunoglu, A., & Hancin-Bhatt, B. (1993). Spanish–English bilingual children's use and recognition of cognates in English reading. *Journal of Reading Behavior, 25*(3), 241–259.

Nation, I. S. P. (1990). *Teaching and learning vocabulary*. New York, NY: Newbury House.

National Assessment Governing Board. (2008). *Reading framework for the 2009 national assessment of educational programs.* Washington, DC: U.S. Government Printing Office.

National Council for Social Studies. (2013). *National curriculum standards for social studies: Chapter 2—The themes of social studies.* Retrieved from http://www.socialstudies.org/standards/strands

National Governors Association Center for Best Practices & The Council of Chief State School Officers. (2010a). *Common core state standards for English language arts and literacy in history/social studies, science, and technical subjects.* Washington, DC: Authors. Retrieved from http://www.corestandards.org/ELA-Literacy

National Governors Association Center for Best Practices & Council of Chief State School Officers. (2010b). *English language arts Appendix A.* Washington, DC: Authors. Retrieved from http://www.corestandards .org/assets/Appendix_A.pdf

National Governors Association Center for Best Practices & The Council of Chief State School Officers. (2010c). *English language arts Appendix B.* Washington, DC: Authors. Retrieved from http://www .corestandards.org/assets/Appendix_B.pdf

National Research Council. (2013). NGSS Lead States. *Next Generation Science Standards: For States, By States.* Washington, DC: The National Academies Press.

Neal, J. C., & Moore, K. (1992). The Very Hungry Caterpillar meets Beowulf in secondary classrooms. *Journal of Reading, 35,* 290–296.

Nesbit, J. C., & Adesope, O. O. (2006). Learning with concept and knowledge maps: A meta-analysis. *Review of Educational Research, 76,* 413–438.

Numeroff, L. (2002). *If you take a mouse to school.* New York, NY: Laura Geringer Books.

Olson, J. K., & Mokhtari, K. (2010). Making science real. *Educational Leadership, 67*(6), 56–62.

Park, E., & King, K. (2003). *Cultural diversity and language socialization in the early years* (ERIC Digest). Washington, DC: Center for Applied Linguistics.

Partnership for Assessment of Readiness for College and Careers. (August, 2012). *PARCC model content frameworks: English language arts/Literacy, Grades 3–11, version 2.0.* Retrieved from www.parcconline.org /sites/parcc/files/PARCCMCFELALiteracyAugust2012_FINAL.pdf

Pavlak, C. M. (2013). "It is hard fun": Scaffolded biography writing with English learners. *The Reading Teacher, 66*(5), 405–414.

Pearson, P., & Hiebert, E. (2013). Understanding the Common Core State Standards. In L. Mandel Morrow, K. Wixson, & T. Shananhan (Eds.), *Teaching the Common Core Standards for English language arts 3–5* (pp. 1–21). New York, NY: Guilford Press.

Piaget, J., & Inhelder, B. (1969). *The psychology of the child.* New York, NY: Basic Books.

Plasket, Kelli. (2012, October 15th). *Mission: Space Jump.* Time for Kids. Retrieved from http://www .timeforkids.com/news/mission-space-jump/53181

Plevyak, L., & Arlington, R. (2012). Kindergarteners, fish, and worms . . . Oh my! *Science & Children, 51,* 54–59.

Possick, J. (2007). An artful forest: A month-long integrated science project teaches primary students about animals and science inquiry. *Science & Children, 45,* 30–32.

Prain, V., & Hand, B. (2006). Language, learning and science literacy. In K. Appleton (Ed.), *Science teacher education for the elementary school.* New York, NY: Lawrence Erlbaum.

Pringle, R., & Lamme, L. L. (2005). Using picture storybooks to support young children's science learning. *Reading Horizons, 46,* 1–15.

Ramer, H. (2013, June 7). 234 years later, New Hampshire slaves are granted freedom. *The Free-Lance Star.* Retrieved from http://www.freelancestar.com/2013-06-08/articles/10429/234-years-later-new -hampshire-slaves-are-granted-freedom/

Rampey, B. D., Dion, G. S., & Donahue, P. L. (2009). *NAEP 2008 trends in academic progress* (NCES 2009-479). Washington, DC: National Center for Education Statistics, Institute of Education Sciences, U.S. Department of Education.

Raphael, T. E. (1984). Teaching learners about sources of information for answering comprehension questions. *Journal of Reading, 28,* 303–311.

Robbins, C., & Ehri, L. C. (1994). Reading storybooks to kindergartners helps them learn new vocabulary words. *Journal of Educational Psychology, 86,* 54–64.

Rohrbeck, C. A., Ginsburck-Block, M., Fantuzzo, J., & Miller, T. (2003). Peer assisted learning interventions with elementary school students: A meta-analytic review. *Journal of Educational Psychology, 95,* 240–257.

Rose, D., & Acevedo, C. (2006). Closing the gap and accelerating learning in the middle years of schooling. *Literacy Learning: The Middle Years, 14*(2), 32–45.

Rose, D., & Martin, J. R. (2012). *Learning to write, reading to learn; genre, knowledge and pedagogy in the Sydney school.* London, England: Equinox.

Roskos, K., & Neuman, S. (2013). Common core, commonplaces, and community teaching and reading. *The Reading Teacher, 66,* 469–473.

Ruiz-Primo, M. A., & Furtak, E. M. (2006). Informal formative assessment and scientific inquiry: Exploring teachers' practices and student learning. *Educational Assessment, 11,* 205–235.

Ryder, J. (1988). *The snail's spell.* New York, NY: Puffin Books, The Putnam Group.

Saunders, W. M., & Goldenberg, C. (1999). *The effects of instructional conversations and literature logs on the story comprehension and thematic understanding of English proficiency and limited English proficient students.* Santa Cruz, CA: Center for Research on Education, Diversity & Excellence.

Saunders, W., & Goldenberg, C. (2010). Research to guide English language development instruction. In California Department of Education (Ed.), *Improving education for English learners: Research-based approaches* (pp. 21–81). Sacramento, CA: California Department of Education.

Scarcella, R. (2003). *Academic English: A conceptual framework* (Technical Report 2003). University of California Linguistic Minority Research Institute (UCLMRI), p. 1.

Scarcella, R., & Merino, B. (2005). Teaching in to English learners. *University of California Linguistic Minority Research Institute Newsletter, 14*(4).

Schleppegrell, M. J. (2004). *The language of schooling: A functional linguistics perspective.* Mahwah, NJ: Lawrence Erlbaum.

Schleppegrell, M. J. (2012). Academic language in teaching and learning: Introduction to the special issue. *The Elementary School Journal, 112*(3), 409–418.

Schleppegrell, M. J. (2013). The role of metalanguage in supporting academic language development. *Language Learning, 63*(1), 153–170.Schleppegrell, M. J., & Achugar, M. (2003). Learning language and learning history: A functional linguistics approach. *TESOL Journal, 12*(2), 21–27.

Schleppegrell, M. J., Achugar, M., & Oteíza, T. (2004). The grammar of history: Enhancing content-based instruction through a functional focus on language. *TESOL Quarterly, 38,* 67–93.

Schleppegrell, M. J., & de Oliveira, L. C. (2013). *An integrated language and content approach for history teachers.* Manuscript submitted for publication.

Scholastic Reference. (2002). *Scholastic children's dictionary.* New York, NY: Scholastic.

Shepard, L. A. (2000). The role of assessment in a learning culture. *Educational Researcher, 29*(7), 4–14.

Silverman, R. D. (2007). Vocabulary development of English-language and English-only learners in kindergarten. *The Elementary School Journal, 107*(4), 365–383.

Simon, S. (1988). *Volcanoes.* New York, NY: HarperCollins Publishers.

Simon, S. (2006). *The heart: Our circulatory system.* New York, NY: Harper Collins.

Snow, C. E., & Uccelli, P. (2009). The challenge of academic language. In D. R. Olson & N. Torrance (Eds.), *The Cambridge handbook of literacy* (pp. 112–133). Cambridge, NY: Cambridge University Press.

Spycher, P. (2007). Academic writing of adolescent English learners: Learning to use "although." *Journal of Second Language Writing, 16*(4), 238–254.

Spycher, P. (2009). Learning academic language through science in two linguistically diverse kindergarten classes. *The Elementary School Journal, 109*(4), 359–379.

Spycher, P. (2013). Meaning-based approaches to literacy education. In B. Irby, G. Brown, R. Lara-Alecio, & S. Jackson (Eds.), *The handbook of educational theories* (pp. 445–458). Charlotte, NC: Information Age.

Stauffer, R. G. (1969). *Directing reading maturity as a cognitive process.* New York, NY: Harper & Row.

Stone, C. A. (1998). Should we salvage the scaffolding metaphor? *Journal of Learning Disabilities, 31,* 409–413.

Swain, M. (2000). The output hypothesis and beyond: Mediating acquisition through collaborative dialogue. In J. Lantolf (Ed.), *Sociocultural theory and second language learning* (pp. 97–114). Oxford, England: Oxford University Press.

Swanson, H. L., & Lussier, C. M. (2001). A selective synthesis of the experimental literature on dynamic assessment. *Review of Educational Research, 71,* 321–363.

Teemant, A., & Hausman, C. S. (2013). The relationship of teacher use of critical sociocultural practices with student achievement. *Critical Education, 4*(4). Retrieved from http://ojs.library.ubc.ca/index.php/criticaled/article/view/182434

TESOL International Association. (2006). *PreK–12 English language proficiency standards.* Alexandria, VA: Author.

Tharp, R. G., Doherty, R. W., Echevarria, J., Estrada, P., Goldenberg, C., Hilberg, R. S., & Saunders, W. M. (2003, March). *Research evidence: Five standards for effective pedagogy and student outcomes* (Technical Report No. G1). Manoa, HI: Center for Research, Education, Diversity and Excellence. Retrieved from http://crede.berkeley.edu/research/crede/products/print/occreports/g1.html

Tharp, R. G., & Gallimore, R. (1988). *Rousing minds to life: Teaching learning, and schooling in social context.* Cambridge, England: Cambridge University Press.

Trelease, J. (2013). *Read-aloud handbook* (7th ed.). New York, NY: Penguin.

Trelease, J. (2014). *Jim Trelease home page.* Retrieved from www.trelease-on-reading.com

Tsang, W. K. (1996). Comparing the effects of reading and writing on writing performance. *Applied Linguistics, 17,* 210–233.

Uccelli, P. (2012, October). *Towards defining and assessing academic language.* Paper presented at the Center for Research on the Educational Achievement and Teaching of English Language Learners (CREATE) Conference, Orlando, FL.

Vacca, J. S. (2008). Using scaffolding techniques to teach a social studies lesson about Buddha to sixth graders. *Journal of Adolescent & Adult Literacy, 51,* 652–658.

Valdés, G., Capitelli, S., & Alvarez, L. (2011). *Latino children learning English: Steps in the journey.* New York, NY: Teachers College Press.

Van de Pol, J., Volman, M., & Beishuizen, J. (2010). Scaffolding in teacher student interaction: A decade of research. *Educational Psychology Review, 22,* 271–296.

van Lier, L., & Walqui, A. (2012). Language and the common core state standards. *Commissioned papers on language and literacy issues in the Common Core State Standards and Next Generation Science Standards, 94,* 44.

Venezia. M. (2009). *Charles Drew: Doctor who got the world pumped up to donate blood.* New York, NY: Scholastic.

Vygotsky, L. S. (1962). *Thought and language.* Cambridge, MA: MIT Press.

Vygotsky, L. (1978a). *Mind in society: The development of higher psychological processes.* Cambridge, England: Cambridge University Press.

Vygotsky, L. (1978b). Interaction in learning and development. In M. Cole, V. John-Steiner, S. Scribner, & E. Souberman, (Eds.), *Mind in society: The development of higher psychological processes* (pp. 79–92). Cambridge: Harvard University Press.

Wells, G. (1996). Using the tool kit of discourse in the activity of learning and teaching. *Mind, Culture and Language, 3,* 74–101.

Wiggins, G., & McTighe, J. (2005). *Understanding by design* (expanded 2nd ed.). Alexandria, VA: ASCD.

WIDA: World-class Instructional Design and Assessment. (2014). Retrieved from http://www.wida.us

Wong Fillmore, L., & Fillmore, C. (2012, January). *What does text complexity mean for English learners and language minority students?* Paper presented at the Understanding Language Conference, Stanford, CA.

Wood, D., Bruner, J., & Ross, G. (1976). The role of tutoring in problem solving. *Journal of Child Psychology and Psychiatry, 17,* 89–100.

Wood, K. D., & Tinajero, J. (2002). Using pictures to teach content to second language learners. *Middle School Journal, 33*(5), 47–51.

Wood, R. (2013, June 7). *234 years later, 20 enslaved revolutionary war veterans are granted freedom.* New Hampshire Public Radio: New Hampshire News. Retrieved from http://www.nhpr.org/post/234-years-later-20-enslaved-revolutionary-war-veterans-are-granted-freedom

Zembal-Saul, C., McNeill, K., & Hershberger, K. (2013). *What's your evidence? Engaging K–5 students in constructing explanations in science.* Upper Saddle River, NJ: Pearson Education.

Zuengler, J., & Miller, E. R. (2006). Cognitive and sociocultural perspectives: Two parallel SLA words? *TESOL Quarterly, 40,* 35–58.

Also Available From TESOL

More Than a Native Speaker

and

From Language Learner to Language Teacher
Don Snow

✳ ✳ ✳ ✳ ✳

TESOL Classroom Practice Series
Maria Dantas-Whitney, Sarah Rilling, and Lilia Savova, Series Editors

✳ ✳ ✳ ✳ ✳

Language Teacher Development Series
Thomas S. C. Farrell, Series Editor

✳ ✳ ✳ ✳ ✳

New Ways in TESOL Series
Jack C. Richards, Series Editor

✳ ✳ ✳ ✳ ✳

TESOL Language Curriculum Development Series
Kathleen Graves, Series Editor

✴ ✴ ✴ ✴ ✴

TESOL Standards

- *Preparing Effective Teachers of English Language Learners:*
  Practical Applications for the TESOL P–12 Professional Teaching Standards

- *Standards for Adult Education ESL Programs*

- *Standards for ESL/EFL Teachers of Adults*

- *TESOL Technology Standards: Description, Implementation, Integration*

- *PreK–12 English Language Proficiency Standards*
  Augmentation of the World-Class Instructional Design and
  Assessment (WIDA) Consortium

  English Language Proficiency Standards

To Order or Request a Review Copy

Online: www.tesol.org "Read and Publish"

Email: tesolpubs@brightkey.net

Toll Free Phone: +1 888-891-0041 (United States)

Mail: TESOL Publications, 9050 Junction Drive

Annapolis Junction, MD 20701 USA